Anthology 2024

Bayside Writers' Group

Copyright © 2024
Bayside Writers' Group
All Rights Reserved
978-0-6455853-7-7   Anthology 2024
978-0-6455853-8-4   Anthology 2024 EBook

This publication may not be reproduced, stored in a retrieval system, or transmitted in whole or in part, in any form or by any means, electronic, mechanical, photocopying, recording, or otherwise without the consent of the author(s). Inquiries should be addressed to the publisher.

Published in Australia
Printed by Ingram Spark

Anthology 2024

Authors: Amanda Divers, Ann Simic, Anna Auditore, Anne Sedgley, David Mills, Dianne Motton, Dita Gould, Ed Davis, Gavan Lintern, Jennifer Baker, Jenny Chevalier, Judith E Dowling, Lisa Westhaven, Lorraine Doney, Lucy Tomov, Monika Nuesch, Peter Levy, Rose Lumbaca Crane, Roslyn Evans, Sandra Lanteri, Sara Vidal, Sharon Hurst, Warren Fineberg, Zhiling Gao

Design: Sharon Hurst
Cover photograph by Freepik (www.freepik.com)

Acknowledgements

Once again, I would like to thank all those who took the effort to submit their works to us. The group has had a very successful year, with increasing membership and lively discussion at all meetings.

We have engaged in readings at various aged care and retirement facilities, which have been met with great appreciation.

Many thanks to The Brighton Library for generously hosting our meetings and giving great support to the group.

Please note that if anyone would like to join the group, make contact with any of our writers in this collection, or wish to be involved in future editions, please email:

baysidewritersgroup@bigpond.com

Contents

Amanda Divers
- Blossom 22
- Sisters 52
- 365 90
- Golden 105
- 16,903.84 146

Ann Simic
- Futile 26
- Kintsugi 51
- Whenever the table 93
- War vigil 121
- Day's end 127

Anna Auditore
- The exhibition 78

Anne Sedgley
- Butcher's Creek, Metung 23
- Spring River crossing 124

David Mills
- Closer every day 1

Dianne Motton
- The Middle East 1977: Jerusalem 28
- The day 87

Dita Gould
- Give me your hand 20
- Stone soup 94
- The power of helping 122

Ed Davis
- The etiquette conundrum 69

Gavan Lintern
    The memorist 46

Jennifer Baker
    Reflection 45
    Unbreakable 68
    Surrounded by others I feel alone 95
    So this is love, I think silently out loud 123
    Into me I see 142

Jenny Chevalier
    The bridge 34
    Globalisation! 106
    The intriguing life story of Madame Dulac 128

Judith E Dowling
    So what! 10

Lisa Westhaven
    Unravelled 53

Lorraine Doney
    The 'A' word 76

Lucy Tomov
    Dark secret 21
    Modernity 33
    Surgery 111
    The absolute limit 120
    How to exist 143

Monika Nuesch
    From Switzerland to Melbourne: an unconventional love story 60

To my precious mother 92
Bliss of declutter 118

Peter Levy
Temptation 86
Secrets of love 149

Rose Lumbaca Crane
How to convey the depths of a life 27
Gaps in sky 44
What helps people? 91
Swimming deeper for the real jewels 110
My English teacher 147

Roslyn Evans
In plain black and white 43

Sandra Lanteri
Broken Dreams 19
Perception 63
Lost in Transition 85
Waiting 112
Music 144

Sara Vidal
Endless blue 64

Sharon Hurst
Haiku for a frangipani 123
The little things 148

Warren Fineberg
A wartime letter of love and loss 114

Zhiling Gao
Orbit 8
Power seizing fiasco – 1967 96

Closer every day

Mist all but obscured the airfields' maintenance hangers, the slight breeze making it swirl as if a ghostly apparition was dancing around the shrapnel scarred buildings. The dense air helped carry the distant sounds of the repairs being made on the squadron's aircraft. The intermittent drilling, hammering and clatter of metal tools dropped on concrete floors were the only sounds that morning to compete with the incessant ringing in his ears.

Last night had been another long sortie, perhaps not the longest of the recent days of bombing raids, but fatigue was taking its toll. Leaning on the rear wall of the mess hall's tin-clad exterior, he looked at the cigarette in his hand as it slowly smouldered towards its extinction, knowing it would quickly be replaced by another. The subtle but uncontrollable shaking made the small smoke plume of the Woodbine quiver as it left the tip.

He drew the crisp morning air deep into his lungs, held it for a few moments then exhaled slowly, hoping this would dissipate the ever-present tension he felt in his gut. The smell of fuel, hydraulic oil and the metallic odour of fresh blood had enveloped him during last nights' raid on Berlin. The contrast with the fresh Cambridgeshire morning made him feel as if he existed in two different worlds. One day closer to this tour being done, he thought.

He dropped his cigarette and mashed it into the ground

with the heel of his sheepskin-lined flying boot. He wasn't that hungry, breakfast could wait. Turning up the collar of his uniform jacket against the chill, he strode across the dew-laden grass towards the infirmary, just to the east of the sandstone Operations building. He resisted the temptation to light another smoke, the rationed tobacco being in short supply and a strict 'no smoking' policy within the infirmary that was just 150 yards away.

A pair of Austin K2 ambulances sat idle on the gravel concourse outside the two conjoined Nissen huts, named after the army engineer who invented them in the First World War. Those, and a small red cross over the entrance doorway, were the only clues to the hut's purpose amongst a plethora of similar buildings on the airfield. The olive-green timber doors showed raw patches where hands had worn the paint away. They swung inwards with a protesting squeal from the rusting hinges as he entered. Bare plywood walls and a single light bulb hanging from the ceiling were uninviting, a small timber bench pushed up against the front wall the only furniture. The warmth from the small wood-burning stove in the entryway instantly made his chilled cheeks tingle and he took the welcome opportunity to briefly thaw his hands.

The surgical ward door swung open behind him and, as he turned from the heater, he saw her. Catherine.

Her name was all he really knew about her. That, and according to his mate Derek, she was one of four new nurses on the base. Two nights ago, he had spotted her across the noisy, smoke-filled bar at The Royal Oak, a favourite pub of the aircrew and just a half-mile from the airfield's main gates. Her floral print dress and cream cardigan were plain and unflattering, her chestnut hair parted, pinned and lightly brushing her shoulders. Maybe it was the fact he was a fair few pints into the evening, maybe something else, but the way she smiled and tilted her head as she chatted with other drinkers had captured his attention. He had convinced himself that she held his gaze for just that fraction too long to be disinterested. His thoughts however, had been cut short by Johnny slapping him on the shoulder and shoving yet another pint of Barclay's stout into his empty hand, excess froth ejecting from the glass onto his uniform sleeve.

"Stop staring, you look like a seagull at the beach waiting for a chip. Come on, we're having the toast for them now, out in the annex."

'Them' were the crews who hadn't made it back from Thursday's operation to the Ruhr Valley targets. Four of the squadron's Lancasters had failed to return, twenty-eight men, their fate not yet confirmed. Statistics would say they were most likely dead. Those in the annex hoped otherwise as they'd lifted their pints in the traditional optimistic toast to a happier outcome. He'd looked around at the others, doing his best to focus. All of them young, all tired, all knew the missing twenty-eight, as did he. Tomorrow is bloody-well promised to no-one, he'd mused to himself, as another mouthful of stout thickened the numbing haze that enveloped him.

"Good morning, Flight-Sergeant." Catherine's cheery greeting brought him sharply back into the present moment.

He felt a twinge of disappointment that she showed no sign of recognition, quickly breaking her fleeting eye contact as she strode past him to a door marked with a small hand-painted 'Storeroom' sign. Her accent was Welsh and he felt somewhat buoyed by the fact that he now knew just that little bit more about her. She was through the door and gone before he could even muster a 'Hello'. He returned to his hand warming, hoping she would reappear as quickly as she had vanished. To his disappointment, a markedly less friendly voice came from behind him.

"And what can I do for you this morning young man?" queried Matron Margaret Appleton, her tone leaving him in no doubt that she ran a no-nonsense facility. No prizes for guessing how the 'ice maiden' nickname had come about, he thought.

"I've come to check on Freddy, Freddy Thorington."

"This way!" she curtly directed as she made a bee-line for the General ward.

He followed her through a pair of plywood swing doors. Ten standard RAF single beds lined each side of the arch-roofed space. A larger version of the foyer's wood heater sat in the centre of the room, doing an adequate job of radiating some warmth. Half a dozen windows, all desperately in need of a clean, filtered in the morning's subdued light. His nostrils were immediately assaulted by the pungent odour of bleach, combined with a trace of something quite unpleasant that he wished had remained inside whomever it came from. Five steps in and the matron abruptly stopped, causing him to make a quick sidestep to avoid what he was sure would be a most unappreciated collision.

"Second last on the left, don't be long, he's weak."

"I understand, thank-you," he replied, as she turned on her heel and made her exit.

He could see Freddy's dark mop of hair and distinctive chin before he'd taken a step toward the bed. It was a relief to find his mate in General, that must be a good sign surely, he thought. As he approached the bed, he could see Freddy's eyes were closed, a large white gauze pad secured with tape to the right side of his face. Numerous small cuts peppered his jawline and chin, most now with a protective scab starting to form. The rectangular chalkboard behind the bed simply read 'Thorington'. A small glass bottle, half-filled with what appeared to be blood, hung from a metal stand beside the bedhead. A plastic tube carried the red fluid down and under the bedcovers, where he assumed it was being delivered via a needle in Freddy's arm. The timber shelf next to the bed had a well-worn surface and held a small white enamel kidney-shaped dish, a roll of fresh bandage and medical scissors within it.

The rhythmic, slow breathing of his sleeping friend somewhat calmed his concerns. Freddy had been in a bad way the last time he had seen him. The cannon shell from the night fighter had hit the rear gun turret just above and to the right of Freddy's head. Fortuitously, it had struck the metal support frame for the turret's perspex dome, otherwise it would have been a quick and messy end to Freddy's twenty-three years on the planet. The shell had fragmented, one large piece ricocheting downward and into Freddy's right leg, the others embedding themselves in the turret's flimsy doors behind his back. Shattered perspex shards had hit his face, his flying goggles saving his sight.

There had been a lot of blood when the wireless operator had pulled Freddy from the turret into the rear fuselage of the Lancaster. Several combat dressings were quickly located in the first aid kit and applied around the metal protruding from Freddy's upper thigh, a shot of morphine seemed ineffective in dulling his pain. He had looked deathly pale as he was loaded into the ambulance after landing back at the base in the early hours of the morning.

Dr George Stewart had been an RAF doctor since the start of the war, temporarily stepping away from a thriving private practice in Hammersmith to 'do his bit' for the war effort. He stopped at the foot of Freddy's bed, picking up the clipboard hanging there and casting an eye over the attached medical chart.

"Good morning, are you one of Freddy's crew mates?"

"Yes, been with him since the start, how's he doing?" he queried.

"He's a lucky young man. The piece of shell in the leg only nicked the femoral artery. If it had severed it I'm afraid the blood loss would have been too much for him to cope with. The surgeon did a fine job of patching him up."

"He was whiter than these bedsheets when we got back, to be honest I was expecting the worst."

"We'll need to fully assess the damage to the leg but I'm hopeful he'll be walking out of here in a week or so."

The brief conversation had been loud enough to bring Freddy out of his slumber. His eyes half-opened and slowly scanned the room before focusing on his bedside companions.

"Well, I can't be dead because you definitely don't look like no angel." he said slowly in his South Yorkshire drawl.

"The doc was just telling me he can't perform miracles with your looks either, but your leg is going to be ok. How are you feeling Freddy?"

"Me leg's bloody sore, doesn't half throb."

"I'm not surprised, you brought home a chunk of German metal in it"

"The other boys alright?" Typical Freddy, always thinking

of anyone but himself.

"Yes Freddy, all good. They'll be in to see you later today too."

Dr Stewart finished making some notes on Freddy's paperwork and slid his pen back into the breast pocket of his white medical coat.

"Get as much sleep as you can Freddy. I'll send a nurse in with something to ease the pain and help you rest."

Taking his cue from the doctor, he reassuringly patted Freddy on the shoulder.

"I'll be back later ok chum, you take it easy."

As he made his way out of the infirmary a wave of tiredness rolled over him, causing a yawn that seemed to arise from the deepest core of his body. The warming sun was slowly dissipating the morning mist and glimpses of blue sky were appearing. A large flock of sparrows noisily darted overhead toward the woodlands to the north, their chirps startling him as he made his way to his barracks.

Freddy, although injured, had been lucky, he thought. They had all been lucky up to this point, some minor aircraft damage on a few ops, but so far they'd made it back from all twenty-eight missions over enemy territory. An urge to light a cigarette invaded his thoughts, pushed aside by the more pressing need for sleep. Climbing into his bed, he silently said his habitual small prayer, giving thanks for his life when so many he knew had given theirs. As sleep overcame him like a heavy morning fog, he pictured Catherine and smiled.

David Mills

Orbit

When the city lights dimmed
And all the storefronts shut down
I roamed down Beale Street
And in the air, a cello's echo whispered,
its notes swaying with the breeze
A gold-rimmed guitar appeared like magic
"I'm the King," a voice boomed, "who are you?"
"This is my Lucille! Damn you, woman!"

"I was just a kid when I read about Martin Luther King."
"I want to see where they took his life.
I heard it's on Main Street."
"Move on, little girl, The Thrill Is Gone!"

A figure danced, twisting and turning with a groovy flair
His white jacket gleamed with every move
"I'm the King, thank you very much," he sang
"Oh, I heard your Love Me Tender during my first love,
though it was forbidden"
"Many things were forbidden here too"
"I'm heading to the Lorraine Motel to catch a glimpse of Martin Luther King"
"Let's walk hand in hand If I Can Dream"

A kid in a black cap, baggy jeans, and a long tee
floated by like he was gliding on water
Spinning on his sneakers, limbs moving like a dream
But he was very real
"Are you a King too?"
"Yo, what's up? I'm Lil Buck, a Memphis jookin' dancer, a different art form."

"You're the dancer from Orbit with Yo-Yo Ma, right?"
"Oh yeah, I danced with him in Beijing. Do you know him?"
"Wish I did, but I love that cello solo piece he did, Orbit by Philip Glass"

As the city lights flickered back to life
And all the storefronts reopened
Beale Street faded behind me
"I didn't make it to see the motel where Martin Luther King was assassinated.
And you didn't remind me," I said to my friend
"Who would have guessed a girl from Inner Mongolia would know about Martin Luther King?"

Zhiling Gao

So what!

The best thing to do was to stay on the right side of Daph. Her temper could flare like a cigarette lighter, and her voice could rise from a resonant alto to a she-wolf snarl in the time it took to thump down a fist. Abuse could flow, in phrases more suitable for a disembowelment than the theft of a banana from the kitchen. Daph would abide no nonsense, she exuded authority, demanded respect and instilled fear. When she entered the room, everyone awaited orders. Her opinions were unarguable, she was always, always right. She knew it and we knew it.

Eighteen stone is a fine weight for a lady. How is it so often that large women can be so light on their feet, so daintily fingered, so soft-skinned? Daph had an enviable complexion, fine and pink. Her silver-grey hair waved off her face from an exaggerated widow's peak. All year round she wore floral cotton dresses with pastel-coloured cardigans stretched over the bodice. These stayed well in place extended around the huge bumps of her breasts. Her upper arms ballooned out at her elbows, though her forearms were average size and her hands were small as a child's. Her feet appeared as castors at the base of tree stump legs.

'Who are these blighters always getting into my kitchen?' she called to sundry people as she elbowed her way to the office at the Nerida Recreation Centre. In one hand she brandished a soup ladle, in the other, an egg lifter. 'I'll throttle them, I tell you!'

A woman flattened herself against the wall to let Daph pass. 'Sorry,' said the woman for no reason at all, then scuttled away.

'Where are my flaming scissors?' Daph yelled at the three staff in the office. 'Who the hell stole my scissors?'

Up off their chairs, the office girls were herded into the kitchen. Daph's size enveloped a chair as she sat, elbows on the table, watching them search for the scissors.

We met, fortunately not physically, as I was ever conscious of the fact that I also might be told to 'Get your bloody carcass out of the way!', each week at the Centre. I moved in trepidation of her for several weeks. She seemed to be many things I was not: confident; organised; influential. I viewed her from afar, studied her as she rattled and clanged about in the kitchen, her kitchen. Each Thursday she concocted a wonderful heartily non-healthy three course meal for all those class participants who find such old favourites as thick pea soup, roast beef and apple crumble, irresistible. Daph thrived on compliments and her cooking was deserving of them. She knew it and we knew it.

Cooking is an Art. Getting food from market to table is a Fine Art. Providing a meal for thirty paying customers single-handed takes a special talent. Daph had a way of bringing my inadequacies to the surface. She ruled from her kitchen with the authority of a hospital matron. As I carefully manoeuvred food from tray to café table without mishap, I wondered how this woman could think of and act on so many things at once. I watched her, she was chopping, she was stirring, she was carving, washing, serving, stacking. I prepared for my afternoon English class; it seemed so insignificant, so unremarkable by comparison.

For weeks I nodded politely, 'Hello' and she did the same. Once I saw her in the office reclining in an armchair dictating her food order for the next week.

'. . . and get four big bags of potatoes, I'm nearly out, and a couple of cauliflowers. Three bunches of silver beet, fresh, and tell them to deliver on time this week, or else!' Daph delegated responsibility calmly and cleverly, with some help from 'Tot', her daughter, an almost pretty but resentful and petulant schoolgirl.

'Mum was wondering …' I was surprised to see Tot at the door of my room. 'Mum was wondering…'

'Oh yes,' I said, 'Mum was wondering…

'Well actually, she wasn't… she didn't…

'She wasn't wondering, she didn't wonder about what?'

'It's me, I was wondering.'

'About what?'

'Well, it's about Mum.' She sat down. 'Could you talk to her, please?'

'I'll talk to her, but about what?' I laughed.

'It's not funny… please.'

'Sorry, how can I help?'

'Help her to read…she can't read, she can't write, she can't add up.'

Tot had the beginnings of her mother's strong character. Her real name was Heather; the Tot came from being the youngest of Daph's eleven children. She was anxious about her schooling, which her mother thought that, now she was nearing fifteen, should come to an end. I understood clearly that Tot was needed at home to help with her father, who was an invalid, and to become a full-time companion to Daph. That was that, no question about it. There was no arguing with her. She knew it and we knew it.

'There's only me left at home now, and Dad,' she told me unhappily.

'Can he help your Mum with her reading?'

'Can't, won't, not these days.'

'So that's your job now?'

'Looks like it,' she shrugged, and tears welled in her eyes, 'Please talk to Mum.'

'I don't think Mum likes me much. It's no good if she doesn't like me.'

'Don't worry, she likes you.'

'How do you know that?'

'She doesn't say bad things about you.'

'Does she know you're telling me this?'

'Not bloody likely, she'd kill me.'

You and me too, Tot, I thought. I could see it vividly, just a horrible, bloody mess on the floor. I visualised Daph with her mop and bucket, wiping us up with much ado. I gave my students a ten-minute exercise, 'My mother and me', whilst I pondered my problem, 'Daph, Me and Tot.'

I knew Daph was a capable cook. She was probably good at many things, but that was the one thing I was sure of. She knew I taught English to mature-age students, so she knew I could read. We had something to offer each other, I thought, as I am a pretty ordinary cook. Then I remembered the Christmas cakes. It had always been a drudge to me, but somehow, I always managed to produce three for family members as a kind of tradition. I felt sure Daph could do a far better job of baking them than I.

At first, I was reticent about asking her. It was at the end of the day when I eventually strode purposefully into her domain.

'Loved the soup, Daph.'

'Yeah, not bad.' She continued to mop the floor.

'It's my favourite, pea and ham.'

'Yeah, not bad.'

'You seem to love to cook, Daph.'

'Yeah, not bad. Out of my way, luv.' Her mop chased me out of the room.

My Christmas cake arrangements were put aside. It was obviously not the right time to ask her. I was angry with myself for being so ridiculously unassertive. Slow, careful, shy, I was so unlike the businesslike Daph.

I got to know Daph over the next three weeks. I did it by behaving in a way which made her comfortable with me.

'Hey Daph, do me a favour, will you?'

She was puffing from polishing the benches.

'Oh yes, what is it?' She didn't look up. 'What is it, people are always wanting….'

'How about making my Christmas cakes for me?'

'It'll cost ya, luv.'

'Don't I know it.'

'I'll fix it up for you. Don't you worry about a thing.'

'Good on you Daph. I'll catch up.'

We discussed the cakes in detail. Daph freely gave advice. She the expert, me the student. I would have to pick them up from her house, she couldn't be expected to deliver them, she told me firmly. Next week, she said, they would be ready next week. I could pick them up on Friday. After four, not before.

Eleven children, I mused, as I walked to her front door. No sign of them now. The spread of her life was now compacted into a small flat. One by one her children had left, each having chiseled chinks out of her, leaving her like an old, adzed tree.

'Martin, the rotten sod, tells me that his girlfriend Lisa's pregnant,' she confided to me the previous week, telling me about her seventh child, her third son.

'I told him just what I think of that.'

'Do you think they'll get married, Daph?'

'Of course. Have to, don't they.'

'What do you think?'

Daph sighed, then brightened. 'She'll make a lovely bride. I'll have to make the bloody dress I suppose. An A-line I think, you know, it'll cover the bump.'

So, Lisa would lack for nothing, no expense would be spared. She would walk down the aisle, swathed and camouflaged in copious yardage of white nylon lace and Daph's own secret would be camouflaged by another of her talents.

Daph opened the door, her bulk filling the space. A large apron failed to cover her shabby, faded dress. Her face seemed scrubbed clean, glowing pearlescent. Her woolly slippers announced to me that my expected visit was not enough to cause a ripple in her day.

'You've come for the cakes,' she informed me gruffly. 'Hang on there.'

I rather liked her straightforwardness; pleasantries can

so often be a waste of time. Tot appeared at the door, chewing on an apple which cracked as she bit into it. She clinked the door latch annoyingly. Her hands were slapped as her mother said, 'Stop that wretched racket.'

I stood at the entrance as Daph went to get the cakes.

'You ask her, tell her about the reading, you said you would, go on,' Tot said in a loud whisper.

I would rather ask a busy employer for a month off on double pay, I thought as I fumbled in my bag for my purse.

'You said you would. You know you said you would.'

She trod hard into the carpet, one foot, then the other, and continued to clink the latch.

The cakes arrived, foil-wrapped on a large tray.

'That's fine.' Daph was not the kind to suffer profuse thanks. I hardly dared touch the heavy silver squares as I felt I could expect a sharp rap on the knuckles.

'I helped,' said Tot. Then she loudly announced, pouting, hands on hips, 'I had to read the bloody recipe.' She stared at her mother, eyes flashing, face reddening. 'Didn't I Mum!'

'I couldn't remember all that, you know, all those bits and pieces."

'I suppose not,' I said inanely, looking at my shoes.

'I have to do it for her all the time.'

'Shut up Tot.' Daph raised her hand, ready to slap, then she let it flop. She crumpled her apron and said, 'I'm not stupid you know.'

'She's not stupid,' Tot said in support, 'She just can't bloody read.'

'So what!' Dot proclaimed to the world.

'So what,' I said, knowing that Tot would continue the conversation.

'So, what are you going to do about it?' Tot stood defiantly, square in front of me.

'Well ... we could see how you go Daph, learning to read and write ... if you like. It's time to think of yourself. I'm sure you'd enjoy it.'

'I've done enough learning,' she said nostalgically.

'Not reading though Mum, not writing ... please ... you can, I know you can.' Tot dragged her hands roughly over her face and left it wet with tear stains.

'It's not a bad idea Daph, we could meet up on Wednesdays after my afternoon class, when you've finished in the kitchen. Let's give it a go.'

'No, not interested. Couldn't care less.'

'Not true Mum, not true.' Tot folded her arms and kicked at the carpet.

'Yeah, yeah, it's not true,' she sighed, 'I never got around to it, just never got around to it.'

'Now Mum! Now! No excuses.'

'Maybe ... maybe I could do it for Tot.'

'For yourself Mum, for you,' she jabbed her mother in the chest and then jabbed herself, 'And for me too.'

'Wednesday, four o'clock,' I said.

'She'll be there.' Tot jumped joyfully, a little girl's jump.

'Cheeky little bugger.' Daph managed a chuckle and pretended to slap Tot.

'She is, isn't she. She's also fantastic.'

'Wednesday at four and that's that.' Tot wagged her finger at her mother.

'Yeah,' said Daph quietly as she handed me the tray.

I walked to my car. Tot had won the day. She was fifteen and years ahead of me. Daph followed me down the path, little light-tripping steps on her hefty legs.

'I suppose I could manage Thursdays too.'

'Fine,' I called.

'I forgot to tell you, the glace cherries, I forgot to put them in the mix.'

'So what, doesn't matter,' I called back.

'It's just that I like to do things properly, not like them at the Centre. You know, I could run that place single-handed, and I'm supposed to be stupid.'

I started the car.

'Now, look here,' she pointed a finger at me and looked stern. 'I don't want to be wasting my time on this reading stuff. If I do something, I do it well, do you see? Wednesday, four. Don't be late.'

Judith E. Dowling

Broken dreams

At midnight
I visited Hopper and Heinwein's Diners
actors, artists, crossing time and space
meeting momentarily on an illusionary stage
before disappearing into memory
All the dark absurdity of it

Monroe, Dean and Pollock were there
lamenting and theorising on their untimely deaths
Elvis pulled a few beers to comfort them

Zelda was crying to Fitzgerald full blast
at not being understood, echoing Van Gogh,
and Bergman was loudly berating Bogart at
having to leave Casablanca

Vivienne was well and truly gone
raving into the wind with Mitchell
and a tubby Brando, in full leather
kept mumbling to Capone about his godfather

conversation wise
these Nighthawks, alone, together
were a dead loss
so I gathered up my living self
and got the hell outa there

Sandra Lanteri

Give me your hand

I lived in Australia for over fifty years with a feeling I didn't belong. When I arrived in 1948, at fourteen, it was because Australia was my parents' choice. I had wanted to go to Israel. At first I was very unhappy. Unlike other children my age, I went to work. First in clothing factories, then to manufacture wafer biscuits in my parents' factory. Doing two shifts from eight in the morning, it was eleven at night by the time I got home. I cried myself to sleep every night for two years. Then I found friends and fulfilment. Life became normal.

Later, in my profession as an art dealer, I had occasion to speak to many cultured people. It upset me when people didn't appreciate our own artists and didn't attend Australian plays. At first I found myself being more patriotic than people born here, yet I still felt alien. When I traveled overseas, I looked for a place to belong, but I no longer felt at home in any European country. At the same time, when I returned home, I was still a foreigner, a 'New Australian' with an accent.

In 2000, I was returning from America by ship to Sydney for The Olympic Games. I had a ticket for the opening ceremony. What excitement! I was staying with friends, and we went to the city for an art opening. Suddenly the guest speaker disappeared. I was told she had gone outside to watch the torch being handed over in the street. I wanted to see this too. The street was full of people and a small woman, like myself, had no chance of seeing over this crowd. I looked longingly at a bench full of people standing up high. A lady looked down; our eyes met. Without a word, she took my hand, stood sideways and pulled me up on the bench. At that moment the torch changed hands in front of our eyes. A feeling, unlike any other, welled up in me and at that moment I became an Australian.

I wish that lady knew what she had done for me. I bless her each time I think of her.

Dita Gould

Dark secret

I mean, it's not really.
Honeysuckled delight; who would call that dark?
We're the path of a spaceship, the air
of a cat. I know I'm not alien but neither
am I real. My hands are foreign in the
early morning and I learn how they work again
stretched out in your garden,
seeking the sun on my lower back.
Lizard warm, tanned feet.
Un-buried, unmoored,
Excavated finally by a secret
so very small,
so very light.

Lucy Tomov

Blossom

On the breeze,
A fleeting blush
Against the sky.
Silent witnesses
To the passage of time,
They bloom
And fall
Without asking
To be remembered.
Yet, for a moment,
They are everything—
Brief as a heartbeat,
Delicate as breath.
The world pauses,
Held in that tender light.
Each petal,
A reminder
Of beauty's impermanence,
Of moments that come and go,
Like spring
Whispering goodbye.

Amanda Divers

Butcher's Creek, Metung

My parents lived at Metung on the Gippsland Lakes, Victoria for over 20 years. They went there for the sailing and the Metung community which was part boating locals, part affluent retirees. It was a cultured community in a beautiful place. Most people have boats - yachts or powerboats for fishing and cruising the Lakes. The village was small, before tourism overtook it: you'd always see people you knew when you went for the morning paper. In Metung you could count on good food, very good wines, friends at the Yacht Club, the little church and the well-known Metung Pub, and a good day out on the water. The rhythms of life in Metung were gracious and ample. It was not a community that felt in need of social change.

One year, my parents took us to a twilight concert in Box's Creek. Box's Creek is a hidden inlet behind a high rocky spur. You could only get there by boat; once anchored, you couldn't be seen from the Lakes. We went in my father's ketch, a 28-foot sailing boat with two masts and a cabin that slept four. The concert was held each year at dusk; people came in every sort of watercraft, mostly yachts and power boats. There was a landing stage on the far side of the inlet where the performers would be. At twilight, all the boats lit up their riding lights - white, red and green - at water level and at mast-tip. The whole inlet sparkled with dancing lights and the sound of popping corks and chinking glass. Then the music began - a solo cello in the darkness. It was magic.

The next year, I asked in the village when the concert would be. "It's cancelled," I was told. "The aborigines won't allow it."

I was told the same thing wherever I asked. "Why?" I asked.

"Dunno. They've forbidden it."

Baffled, I dropped in at Krowathunkoolong, the Bairnsdale Keeping Place, and asked the two young men there what was going on. "It's a sacred place," they said. "A massacre site. So many of our people were killed there." This is the story they told me:

In the mid-19th century, Angus Macmillan, the explorer, had an extensive landholding at Bushy Park, north of Maffra. In 1841 one of the local tribesmen speared one of his cattle. Macmillan's men attacked the warrior and one of the cattlemen was killed. In reprisal, Angus Macmillan vowed to "teach the blacks a lesson" and ordered his men to destroy the whole tribe. The clan fled to the east, men, women and children on foot, running to escape the men on horseback coming after them.

Can you bear to picture it? It is 100 kilometres from the Avon River to the Gippsland Lakes near Metung. Men, women, babies, children and old people, running in terror to the safety of the sacred inlet on Bancroft Bay. Macmillan's men pursued them on horseback across the Perry, the Mitchell, the Nicholson and the Tambo rivers and countless creeks[1]. There were no roads, no bridges. For Macmillan and his men, it would have been an exciting hunt.[2] When they came to the high ridge overlooking the inlet, they shot all the people taking refuge in the water, men and women, old and young. One or two crept away and later told what happened. It was said that not only the inlet but the whole of Bancroft Bay ran red with blood for a week.

It was called Butcher's Creek for years until Judge Box bought land overlooking the inlet and changed its name to Box's Creek. If some of the Metung people knew the true story of Butcher's Creek, they might not condemn the Gunnai-Kurnai people so roundly for cancelling their concert.

Some people I know would simply refuse to believe this story - "if it were true they would have heard of it", etc. etc. But others, hearing this story and hundreds like it across Victoria and Australia, would begin to see that Reconciliation is a two-way process: we have to forgive them for making small demands on us; they have to forgive us for repeated atrocities. Looking beyond what we "know" to find out what they know is the first essential step. There is no other way forward.

Endnotes

[1] Gay Halstead wrote in "The Story of Metung " 1977:

... the stockmen followed closely behind [their two black trackers] as they crossed the Mitchell, Nicholson and Tambo Rivers and they were eventually tracked down by 'the boys' - the trapped offering little resistance to the rain of bullets and being shot down at Butchers Creek on Bancroft Bay.

[2] In an article in the Bairnsdale Advertiser of 2.12.1954, Frank Bury wrote:

The blacks swam all the intervening rivers and made for what they considered to be the best hiding place in their area of Gippsland. They were however trapped and shot down.

These excerpts are quoted from Peter Gardner's excellent history, *Gippsland Massacres: the Destruction of the Kurnai Tribes 1800-1860*, 3rd ed. 1st edition published 1983, pp. 49-50.

Anne Sedgley

Futile

From my perch I peruse tiny black ants.
As they climb the ladder that thrusts to the sky, I spy
their ascent, each clutching one white egg, deposit it
in the first link of the ladder, scurry back, briefly bump
laden ants on their way up.
I warn them it's a hazardous home.
They don't listen.

Precarious: in the worker's jaws, risks abound; a
delicate morsel for many.
What spurred this shift from the nest's
safe dark depths to the dangers of the day?
Was their den too dry, too wet, infested with a fungus.
It's all secret.

But the ladder will be collapsed,
their home in the heights destroyed.
I'm supposed to squash them,
stop their futile labour,
save their future sorrow, but I sit,
calmly contemplate the heft of trifling life.

Ann Simic

How to convey the depths of a life

What will I sculpt now with the last bit of clay?
The tear that fell from one of my mother's eyes
I had never seen my mother cry before, she had many reasons to
She probably cried in private as many people do
She probably cried for how she was treated by others who did not care
Did she cry because she must have missed her family
Did she cry for the love she had for her children
She cried her last cry and it was just one single tear before she left this world
That was the only time I ever saw tears from my mother's eyes and it was just one single tear
She endured anguish, betrayal and worries that manifested into illnesses as they sometimes do
She could not express how she felt, an illness had taken her voice too
How frustrating and sorrowful it must have been for her
How could I put all that in a sculpture, in a piece of artwork that conveys such depths and emotions of a life
So I choose the medium that suits
A way of honoring my mother who was mostly misunderstood
One of the many memories that I have of my mother
The memory of my mother's last tear

Rose Lumbaca Crane

The Middle East 1977: Jerusalem

My husband had been keen to visit Israel. He had just completed a theological degree back home in Melbourne and was to be ordained when we returned from a six-month trip around Europe. He felt that a trip to the ancient cities where Christ had trod would be a moving experience. I had less spiritual hopes, merely wishing to see a place that I had read about in literature and history books for years but never imagined that I would have the chance to see in the flesh. The prospect of eating falafels had its appeal as well!

We had been backpacking around Europe armed with a Eurorail pass each, one spare change of clothes in our pack, many smelly socks and a good deal of enthusiasm to cope with walking for kilometers to find cheap pensiones and even cheaper tourist menus. We interrupted the madness of catching trains at midnight for the luxury of a plane flight from Athens to Tel Aviv on a TWA plane, manned by some of the oldest airline stewardesses I had ever seen. Their version of service was to plonk the orange juice down in front of us, spilling most that they handled and then ignored us for the rest of the flight. They clearly had grown tired of their job.

Sitting next to me was an American man, a thirty something Jewish New Yorker who spent the whole trip panicking about the lack of security at Athens airport and declaring that he hoped we wouldn't be hijacked or bombed out of the sky. I listened patiently to his ravings between mopping up the orange juice, thinking that he was slightly unhinged, until many months later Athens airport was the site of the first spate of plane hijackings in the late 1970s.

On arriving in Jerusalem, we had strict instructions to visit my friend Elly's aunt's house in the old city. Elly had given us an introductory letter to her aunt and some gifts for her. Her aunt lived with her family in the Convent of St.John in the Christian quarter, a well-defined area of the city, accessed through the Jaffa Gate.

As we passed under the high thick wall of the old city, we entered another world, a world devoid of cars and many of the trappings of modern life. A labyrinth of narrow winding streets appeared in front of us, cobbled stone paths leading towards dim alleyways. We had to ask directions and managed to walk past the entrance to the convent three times before realizing it, unable to read the Arabic and Greek writing high on the wall. We stood confused in front of a large steel door until a kind stranger showed us that to access the convent we had to go through the biblical "eye of the needle", a small door within this larger door. We stepped through the doorway emerging into a courtyard surrounded by small dwellings with stairways leading to an upper level.

The house we sought was part of the complex of buildings that made up this convent. Made of sandstone blocks, it dated back hundreds of years, each room with a domed stone roof and stone floor. The toilet was in a small external room and the shower a jerry-rigged set of pipes connected to a solar heating panel on the roof of the dwelling. It was crude but effective, as long as the sun shone. All over the rooftops of Jerusalem and indeed everywhere throughout Israel, encouraged by the government, were these home

-made methods of harnessing solar power. The Israelis seemed determined to make themselves as independent as possible of the need to generate power.

Elly's aunt Stamatia was amazingly generous in her welcome and insisted that we stay with them that night and for what became a week of roaming the old city's ancient sites. The Via Dolorosa, with the Stations of the Cross marked above various doorways, became a well known route for us as we wandered back and forth through the various quarters of Jerusalem - the Jewish area with men dressed in the traditional Hassidic garb and the Arab quarter where we tried to avoid the welcoming entreaties to buy caftans and rugs from street sellers.

Every night, after the family had viewed television, with most programs spoken in Hebrew, we converted the couch in the lounge room into a bed, slept and then packed it up again the next morning. Stamatia insisted on us sharing every meal with the family despite the fact that there were already four mouths to feed and they were a household that did not have an over abundance of material wealth.

My over-indulged Australian sensibilities were acutely challenge one night when dinnertime approached. Some fruit was placed on the table and everyone ate an orange or a banana and then moved off to do whatever chores were required. As I sat eating my piece of fruit, I realized that this was dinner and that my concept of a two to three course meal with at least some meat was not going to happen. I felt further humbled that night when Stamatia gathered all the leftovers from the small fridge and gave her twelve- year old son strict instructions to take them to one of their neighbours, who was struggling to make ends meet.

Every lunchtime, a relative, Uncle, who was the Greek Orthodox Archbishop of Bethlehem, would come to Stamatia's to share a simple meal and chat with her about the family. He had been the archbishop when the Israeli Six Day war began against the Egyptians in 1969 and he had stood on the top of the Church of the Nativity in Bethlehem hosing down the wooden roof from burning embers, as the mortar shelling continued around him.

Despite his exalted position in the church, he had all the appearance of a poor humble man, dressed in a worn black cassock, the fabric faded from too much laundering. Adorning his feet were a simple pair of brown leather sandals, scruffy yet serviceable. His beard was grey and curly, an odd black hair still present, reminiscent of his youth. He would sit at the table, dipping pita bread into his soup or the *stifatho*, occasionally dribbling a bit of food down the front of his cassock. He would encourage me to eat more, pointing at the food in front of us, usually muttering in Greek that I ate like a sparrow.

He had a presence and an air of piety about him, despite the fact that I could not communicate directly with him. He spoke Greek, Hebrew, and Arabic. I felt decidedly uneducated, with only English in my language repertoire. We communicated through Stamatia, each of us waiting patiently for the next piece of the translation.

One day, Uncle kindly offered to take us around the Church of the Holy Sepulchre, the most holy of holy places for a Christian, being the supposed site of Golgotha, the place where Jesus was crucified. Throughout, the church was divided into various areas under the control of the Armenians, Catholics, Syrians, Coptics, Ethiopians and Greek Orthodox. Each denomination had laid claim to part of the church over the centuries and they jealously guarded their territory, watching each other for infringements of behaviour or for trespassing into their own territory. They even charged unsuspecting tourists many Israeli pounds for the right to view another icon or holy spot within their area of the building. However, wherever we went, Uncle waved people aside, striding out in front of us, saving us from any expense. From the cobwebs of my memory came the lessons of Sunday school and the story of the moneychangers in the temple. The irony of watching people charge money to view such a holy site was not totally lost on my near heathen soul.

We spent a second week traveling by bus through other cities of Israel before returning to Athens and my friend's flat to meet her mother, Stamatia's sister. We chatted and happened to mention our meetings with Uncle. I casually mentioned that he had asked us to go to Jordan with him, but that we had refused his kind offer, needing to get back to Europe and use the remaining days of our Eurail passes.

Elly's mother had a horrified expression on her face.

"You what! You didn't accept his offer! Oh, my dear, you are mad!" declared my friend's mother.

"Why? What's the problem? Did we do something wrong?" I asked, thinking that somehow, I had unwittingly made a social gaffe.

"My dear you missed the opportunity of a life time. When Uncle was a young man, there was an assassination attempt on the then King of Jordan. Uncle and another priest sheltered the young Prince Hussein from the bullets and saved his life. Ever since then Uncle has been held in high regard by the Prince, who of course is now the King. Whenever Uncle travels to Jordan he stays as a guest in the palace of King Hussein. You would have stayed there too, as part of Uncle's entourage."

I sat dumbfounded as the true import of what she had said sunk in. I knew the thoughts of Andy Warhol, who claimed that everyone was entitled to their fifteen minutes of fame in life, but I sadly realized that I had been offered one of life's unique opportunities, to be a guest in a royal palace. And I blew it.

Dianne Motton

Modernity

The stark relief
of a loaf of
seedless-flourless-eggless
bread
against footage of
a mother who softly
and
wordlessly covers the
gleaming blistered
skin of her forearm,
before gently pushing her
son's eyelids
closed as he lays
upon the
burnt wreckage
of his bedroom.

Lucy Tomov

The bridge

As far as I can remember, the bridge has been the focus of my whole life. Halfway was the border, which separated our town from another country, for me, another world. A new world I longed to go to someday! A world of freedom, democracy, a world where women like me have rights and were considered human beings, not just chattels. It represented life without 'chains', the rainbow on the horizon. It was just a dream though, as I knew no women would be allowed to cross that bridge, because if only one did, then all the women in our town would have rushed out of the country and over that bridge to escape their miserable lot. Besides, one needed a passport and a special visa issued only by the highest authorities and only on very special circumstances, to be able to reach the coveted other side of the border.

My mother belonged over the bridge as a young girl, before she met my father. He was from our village and had been sent on business to Utopia where my mother lived. They fell in love and got married. After the wedding, as a happy young bride, (she was only 16 years old) she crossed the bridge with her beloved husband looking forward to a life of sheer bliss with the man she loved.

What awaited her in that narrow-minded, primitive society, was a miserable existence. She no longer recognised the man she married. He had become like all the men in Hella, a selfish cruel master who held her as all the women in this town, a prisoner in her own home. That was the custom in this ignorant, backward country. Women were not allowed to show their faces or any part of their anatomy in the street. They were not allowed to leave the house without a male family member. Education was only for the male species, there were no schools for girls. Their only lot in life was to get married, do the household chores, have children and please their lord and master. They totally depended on him. Divorced or widowed women did not have the right to work and earn a living. Oh no! They could starve with their children if there were not some charitable relative who would give them a hand out just to survive. The government washed its hands of the whole matter.

My mother had four children, three boys and one girl, me. I had a twin brother Zino, we were the youngest. My two older brothers, Wady buddy and Sery were now in high school while Zino was in his last year of primary. I stayed home with my mother and helped her with the daily chores. My mother encouraged my brothers, when they came home from school, to teach me everything that they had learnt at school that day, which they did willingly as we were a closely-knit family and I was so eager to learn. My mother also taught me to read and write as she had completed her studies in high school in her country, where no such laws as ours existed with regards to girls' education. I considered myself so lucky in comparison with the rest.

My father never found out about my studies. He would have been so afraid of the consequences if the news filtered out. "What? A girl learning to read and write? That was blasphemy against the religion". That would have been enough to make him lose his job and be shunned by the rest of the male population. So, my studies became our secret.

My mother often talked about Utopia, about her family she was never allowed to visit, friends she left behind, the happy carefree life she used to lead before she married my father. Oh, how she desperately wished to be free to cross the bridge back to her home with us, her children, where she felt she really belonged.

I was lucky to have so many brothers. Sometimes they would take me out with them, covered up from head to foot, of course, and we would walk down the street visiting some shops, the marketplace where they would buy me little trinkets. This would give me a lot of pleasure and I could not wait to show them to my mother. She would smile and hug me, happy to see the joy in my eyes.

I was now fifteen years old and my father was talking of marriage. Girls in this country got married very young, sometimes as young as twelve or even nine, often with much older men. Fifteen therefore was a very ripe old age and the fact that I had escaped this fate earlier was because my father was a businessman, a higher class than a poor employee or a factory worker.

One day, my father came home earlier than usual. He said he had good news for us.

"What good news?" asked my mother.

"The good news concerns our daughter Frie. Can't you guess, Shira?" My mother felt faint.

"Are you saying you found a husband for our daughter already?" she asked.

"What do you mean, already, others her age are already married and with child you know."

"Who is this man?" she started.

"Don't worry. He is a good man who will take very good

care of Frie. He is one of my colleagues at work. He has a very good position and she will lack nothing."

"A colleague of yours? How old is he?" asked Shira.

"He is forty, a good mature age for a man to take care of a household."

"But you were only twenty when we were married, remember?"

"I know, but I was too young to take on the responsibility of a family. I never mentioned it to you but I often felt it."

"Can't we wait a little longer to marry Frie, she is still so young and naive Lery, please?" my mother begged.

"Definitely not! I gave my word to Sully, my colleague; the wedding will take place next month. That will give you enough time to prepare her trousseau and organise the wedding ceremony. Now what's for dinner, Shira? I'm starving."

I had never met my future husband. That was the custom. The father would choose the man to marry his daughter and the girl had no say in the matter whatsoever. Despite my mother's fears, I was curious to meet the man I was going to marry. I even felt quite excited about the whole thing. The wedding ceremony, the entertainment, the new clothes my mother bought me. All this contributed to the novelty of it all.

The wedding day arrived. The whole family, relatives and friends came to help organise the festivities. Tables were set in both rooms as men and women would celebrate separately. The women had cooked the whole day and prepared several delicacies for the guests: pigeons, chickens, ducks prepared with spices and herbs, lamb on the spit, a variety of vegetables and fruit and much more. The sweets, trays and trays of fluffy pastries cakes which would melt in the mouth. On a wedding day, no money was spared for the celebrations. The Father's honour was at stake!

In the early evening the guests started to arrive. The women and men were directed to their respective area. There was a band and a singer performing in each room. Later on in the evening, the dancing girls would join in and the party would then be in full swing with everyone dancing and joining in the singing. Women and men would dance among themselves, of course, no mixing was allowed.

Around 10pm, the groom's mother stood up and asked me to follow her in a special room, as was the custom. There would take place the last phase of the marriage ceremony. The mother, with the use of a handkerchief, would deflower the young girl in order to prove her virginity was intact to everyone there. The handkerchief, covered in blood, would circulate among the guests who would then share the bride in recognition of her innocence. The consequence of the opposite was death, usually performed by the father or a big brother.

My excitement for the celebration waned completely and fear and pain replaced it when I had to undergo the ritual of deflowering. I felt I was treated like an animal and not a human being, having to submit to such a barbaric custom. My mother had tears in her eyes and held me close after I came out of the room, trying to console me, but not finding the words to justify what that just happened. The party continued for another hour when the time came for the groom to come and meet me, his new wife, for the first time and take me to the new home. We were to live with his parents.

When I first laid eyes on my new husband, I gasped; he

looked older than my own father did and so ugly with his fat face and his thick black moustache! All my hopes of a little happiness disappeared and I felt my blood withdrawing from my face, to the despair of my mother, sitting next to me, distressed with a knowledge that there was nothing she could do to save her beloved daughter from the fate that was awaiting her.

Life with my husband resembled my mother's life with my father. My days were taken up with chores. My mother-in-law was not friendly towards me and expected me to do all the work and look after my father-in-law who was very old and needed constant care. Sometimes I wonder whether Sully, my husband, did not marry me just to look after his sick and ageing father and relieve his mother of the burden. He never showed much affection towards me and treated me more like his maid than his wife! I could feel myself sinking day after day into utter despair. I very seldom went out with him as he spent most of his free time after work at the local cafe with his friends.

My mother and brothers would visit me sometimes, but those occasions were rare as my husband did not like my brothers and would forbid me to receive them unless he was present. The times where I could see my family were a highlight of my dull life. I miss them all so much! I always cried for hours after they left and would plunge even into deeper despair. I asked my husband if we could go together sometimes to see my parents. After a lot of pleading, he promised that we could go there once every three months if I behaved myself. He had caught me once reading a book when he came home earlier one evening! Well! I have never seen him in such a state of the bewilderment! He could not believe his eyes! Was that his wife, a woman, reading a book? He came towards me, whisked the book off my trembling hands and slapped my face so hard that I staggered backwards from the shock.

"How come you can read? Tell me the truth now! You want to ruin my reputation?"

I could not utter a word. Then I remembered that luckily the book had illustrations and photographs and I managed to convince him that I was not reading it, but looking only at the pretty pictures!

"Who bought you that book? Your brothers no doubt."

"No, I took it with me when I left home as a souvenir and because I enjoyed looking at the illustrations, that's all," I said.

"Don't let me catch you with a book again, or you will be very sorry. I promise you. Is that understood?"

"Yes, yes, but I get so bored sometimes, can't I keep it just to look at the pictures from time to time, please Sully, I am so often alone."

"And who is going to do all the chores around here? Answer me, who? There is enough work here to keep you busy all day. In the evenings, when I'm not home, you can keep my poor parent's company instead of wasting your time looking at pretty pictures".

He then took the book and tore it in front of my eyes and drop the pieces on the lounge room floor.

"I hope that will serve you as a lesson and that from now on you will behave yourself Frie. Now go to bed, I won't be long. You can sweep the floor tomorrow", he said, when he saw me bending down to pick up the pieces of scattered paper.

I knew why he'd come home early earlier that evening and I dreaded the thought of what was to follow. I dreaded the way life like on our wedding night, when without any regard for me, a new bride still hurting from the barbaric deflowering ritual, he threw his big bulky frame on me and lifting my nightgown, penetrated me ignoring my cries, got his pleasure and went to sleep. I could have been a dummy that he would not have acted any differently. If that was love, I wanted no part of it!

The book incident for me was the last straw! Life was not worth living anymore. I thought of committing suicide, but later relented. How would my dearest mum and beloved brothers feel if I did? No, I had to find another way of escaping this tyranny before I became completely insane.

The day arrived when we were to visit my family. I had to find time to talk with them away from my husband! They had to save me from the wretched life I was leading, but then, I thought, what could they do? The laws of this country were so strict; their hands were tied.

As soon as we reached the front door, we saw my mother, brothers and even my father standing there to greet us as we had advised them of our visit. I threw myself in my mother's open arms, weeping with a joy of seeing her.

"My baby, my poor baby, don't cry, I cannot bear it. Are you so miserable my Frie?" she whispered.

"If you only knew how much, mum, I want so much to get away from him and his parents," I whispered back in her ear.

She held me tight for a second and then let go me to greet my husband and invite us in. Later, the men sat at the table for dinner whereas the women, mum and I, as was the custom when you had male visitors, were to eat in the kitchen. That gave me the chance to pour my heart out. My mother, who had never seen me in such a state before, could do little else then hold me against her, stroking my head, saying "I know, my darling, I know what you are going through. I went through the same feelings too as young bride. One day, however, when you will have children of your own, there will be compensation. You and your brothers have brought me so much joy, that my life has had taken a new meaning and I managed to bear its vicissitudes with more patience and acceptance.

As my mother spoke, I understood that I was doomed; nothing short of a miracle could save me from my present wretched condition and I surely hoped I will not have any children with this horrible man I had married. Oh, how I long to cross that bridge and live as a decent human being, free from my chains. Free to be a woman in my in her own right. Live a normal existence in Utopia as my mother's, before her marriage.

Suddenly, I got up and left the kitchen pretending I was going to the toilet, sneaked out of the house very quietly, ran to my beloved bridge and started to cross it, running towards my deliverance, not stopping at the sound of the soldier's voice crying out, "Halt, who's there?"

It was dark and I hoped they would not see me. I had to be quick and cross to the other side.

I did not stop even when the voice said, "Stop or I'll shoot!"

I continued to run for my life.

"It's a woman! I think she is dead! I did warn her to stop but she continued running towards the border. I could not let her reach the other side. I have no choice; I had to fire!"

At last, I was free.

Jenny Chevalier

In plain black and white

Priceless: "Colonisation has actually been good for
Aboriginal people"
A word from a cleric: "Let's terminate welcome to
country ceremonies"

Trump card: "To vote Yes means division
                To vote No means unity"

Do not go gentle into that dark space
Of living with blind voters' ignorance and hate
Rage, rage against the dying of the race

Though wisest knew to answer Yes was right
Their words had forked no lightning so for now
Our country has descended into night

We must keep fighting justice in this land
Admit that sovereignty has not been ceded
Create a brand new future hand in hand

**Always was, always will be
Aboriginal land**

Roslyn Evans

Gaps in sky

True is the blue in the sky, so vast, so high
I look for the gaps between threatening clouds
The clouds that get in the way, how they make me feel a certain way
Those nasty gray clouds
How to change all that and make me feel better?
The blue in the sky makes me cheerier and warmer
It soothes me so, my body likes it so
The Egyptians worshipped the sun, happier they were, while their crops grew and grew
They understood the laws of the land, the laws from the sky, the invisible right laws
Within the gaps of thoughts and breaths
Truer than the questionable thoughts at times
So many thoughts, repetitive thoughts, oh I thought I was over that, oh it's just another thought
I watch my thoughts, sit in silence for a while and breathe for it is all part of me
I remember to breathe deeply for a while as it makes sense to be with the better thoughts
I take another mindful deep, gentle long breathe
Helping my mind, my body and life
Even the great thinkers think so
So I breathe and I watch for the gaps in the sky between the clouds of gray
How to feel better whether the sky is blue or gray?
I watch the clouds, thoughts, emotions
I watch them drift from my world
How to feel better whether the sky is blue or gray?
Oh yes, I remember I tucked a piece of sun in my heart, in my state of being
and it is there forever, oh there it is

Rose Lumbaca Crane

Reflection

She makes it difficult to love her.
No matter how hard you try.
She's not quite right.
She has a certain look in her eye.
She stares you down, it is her that is meant to look away first.
She begs for attention, you give it, she rejects it.
It's not the love she wants.
She does not know what she wants, yet somehow she expects you to know.
She makes it difficult to love her.
Believe me I have tried.
She is not the cat's mother.
She.
Is.
Me

Jennifer Baker

The memorist

"How do you keep your garden going when everyone else's is dying?"

I looked up from pulling weeds. He was hanging over the fence. Maybe eighteen years old. Final year in high school, I imagined. I had seen him before, always by himself, looking up from the bottom of the hill, as if wondering who lived in the small cottage so different to those wide-verandaed farmhouses that everyone else lived in.

Tuchman stirred from his shady spot. He came over to me, purring, tail up, executing a figure eight through my legs, marking me as his for the stranger, before sitting on his haunches to gaze at my visitor.

"My dad says you have a well, but I don't think so."

I straightened my back, easing out the cricks. Tall. Even standing, I had to look up at him. My bent, ageing back didn't help.

"He says you're not from here. You just got lucky finding a well with water when no one else can. It was probably already there when you moved in."

"Hmmmmm."

"I tell my dad you know something. It's the way you do your garden. When it rains, the water doesn't run off into the creek like everywhere else. It gets trapped by those little bumps and hollows you've done, so the rain soaks in. And that makes things grow better and you never have patches with nothing growing for long and that catches the rain too."

"What does he say to that?"

"He says that's silly. If you were that clever, you'd be out there telling us, showing that you were smarter than us."

He spoke assuredly. Comfortable that he understood how I cared for the land. How I had restored it to its natural state. How I had reversed decades of damage by erosion. Repairing the channels that had carried the precious water straight downhill and away from my garden forever. How I caressed the rain with natural grasses. In the right places, diverting precious moisture to where it could soak in until needed.

"What do you think?"

"No! Adults don't like to be told they are doing something wrong, especially when it's something they've been doing all their lives and especially by an outsider."

That thought struck me. Perceptive for one so young.

He had a way of looking at the world, quizzically, drinking it in, never satisfied that he was taking in enough.

Was he the one? I had expected someone older, a young woman, possibly in her 40s, with enough years yet to live but having lived enough to know a thing or two. It had always been so; women that is, but there was no rule. Had I been looking in the wrong places? I needed a wise soul, but one infected with an inquisitive streak. Possibly, young and male might not be so bad.

Several hundred years I had lived, and now many decades on my own. I was almost ready to leave this world. Could he be the one to carry our remembrances? Could he be the one to maintain our traditions? Could he be the one to carry our spirit to the new generation that would surely reappear somewhere in this world at some time in the future?

"Could I interest you in something to read?" I asked.

His eyes lit up. "I love to read. I've read everything in our school library. There's nothing left for me."

Then a concerned pause. "I have to be home by dinner."

Ah, the practicality of it all!

"Tell your parents. Come back if they say you can. They might not like you talking to the crazy old lady on the hill."

"Yes."

Not even a flicker of surprise that I would refer to myself in such a way. My heart skipped a beat. He seemed right. Could I do this to him? He did not deserve this.

If he came back, he would read. He would come to understand. If he was right, I would not need to suggest or hint. He would know.

~~~

Chibbles stirred on my lap, padding her front paws into my thigh. I gazed down the hill at the young woman leaning over my fence, searching for clues about something in my garden, sometimes glancing up towards me. She had a way of looking at what was around her, searching, pondering. In her own thoughts.

Most people passed without noticing my garden, but she had stopped many times before. Possibly fourteen years old the first time. Even then, tall, lanky for her age. Now in her mid-20s. As tall as I once was. She always stopped when by herself. Never when with someone. Never even glancing my way when with someone.

Years ago, I had left something for her. A fruit or a

vegetable? I don't remember. She had looked up the hill as if asking permission. Then she'd taken it. Now, there was often something for her. I knew when she would come by herself.

My mind wandered back to my own early years. There'd been Tuchman who had outlived his companion, my new friend, by almost a decade. On that first evening Tuchman and I were alone, he'd climbed onto my lap for the first time. Now, it was me he would care for.

In his final weeks, as if understanding the need, Tuchman had brought home a kitten, dishevelled and near death. He and I nurtured that kitten, who recovered and became Coot. One day, soon after Coot had recovered, he called to me from outside. He'd found Tuchman near my old friend. That night, when I settled down to read, Coot took Tuchman's place in my lap. Coot kept me company for a quarter of a century. He found Lindi who, in her final weeks, then found Kaos. There had been others, one after the other, an unbroken chain, with Chibbles the latest link. More cat lifetimes than I cared to count.

Even a few human lifetimes. My garden, once an oasis of green among dry, barren fields, was now an oasis of green among paved roads and elegant townhouses. Lately, there'd been those who saw townhouses where my garden and cottage stood. More money than I'd ever imagined. Money I did not need.

It had been awkward at first. My friends did not understand why I would devote myself to caring for a stranger. A frail, elderly woman so small and bent that some doubted she was human. She'd become my teacher, my mentor, my spiritual guide. When she had passed, my friends encouraged me to find someone and start a family, but by then I understood that was not for me. My friends eventually came to accept that this was my life. They drifted away, some returning after absences of years, even decades, until they too passed.

I remembered the words of my mentor and friend. "One day, many years from now, there will be more of us. I must pass my memories on so that those who are to come may build on them, avoiding the mistakes we made. My life is flowing out of me. Will you share in my memories so that you can pass that wisdom on when it is time?"

For many decades since the last of my own childhood friends had passed, I'd had my feline friends and other ancient friends I'd found in my mentor's library of memories.

I had explored and treasured those books I'd inherited from my mentor, labouring with pen and paper to add my own memories, waiting for the new generation. But even a memorist cannot live forever. I now feared the new generation would not come even in my extended lifetime.

My thoughts returned to the girl, now a young woman. Could I possibly hand my responsibility to another, consign them to the life I had led. I had no regrets, but there had been sufferings mixed in with the joys. Friends and family had aged and passed as I had lived on. More years than I'd ever imagined, with memories of treasured friends who could no longer visit except in my mind.

Could she be the one? Could I impose this on her? I should at least greet her and judge for myself. Then it would be for her to decide.

Gavan Lintern

Kintsugi

When that exquisite large blue and white Arabia plate finally shattered, I reeled; a wedding present, half a century; its end not a marriage in distress.

Gather shards, watered with flashbacks, history; piece them together with golden threads, invoke kintsugi - no less versed for faults.
Reminiscent and differentiated.

This is my plate now; its fate cradling time, returned to life, cherished; recaptured, what it was; a small smile for what it is.

All these years later, a little broken,
pieced together, I am here,
strong and infirm.

Ann Simic

Sisters

Three years between us—
A gap so small,
Yet enough for you to lead
And me to follow.
You were always just ahead,
But close enough to reach.
We grew together,
Like two trees with roots entwined,
Branches stretching in different directions,
Yet always touching.
Your laughter, a mirror of mine,
Your tears, my own.
We shared secrets
In whispered tones,
And dreams that curled around us
Like warm blankets on cold nights.
I knew you better
Than I knew myself,
And you, me.
Through the years,
We carried each other's joys,
Held up one another's fears.
Distance couldn't divide us—
Our hearts always close,
Bound by more than blood
But by love,
Unspoken,
Everlasting.

Amanda Divers

Unravelled

A yarn, that's what they call a good story, isn't it? Have you ever wondered about how I discovered I'm a witch, because it wasn't immediately obvious. I mean look at me, I'm not exactly straight out of witchy central casting, am I? I don't tick any of the sexy-scary-glam-terrifying boxes. Just boringly nondescript – averagely average you'd have to say. Hiding, plain; absolutely no insight about it.

So, anyway, back before I knew I was a witch, I was sitting on the tube commuting to my dullsville job, a weekday like any other. The only bright spot was I'd celebrated the turning of a truly disappointing summer into a chilly autumn by wearing a new jumper. Yes, even in my triumphs I was tedious. I remember looking down at the lambswool blend with the happy expectation of being pleased, but no. There was a loose thread at the side seam. I forget which high street brand was responsible for this lapse in quality control, but I do remember the sense of resignation I felt at their shoddy sweatshop manufacturing. This was all I deserved. I'll never have nice things.

As we all know, the right thing to do when seeing a loose thread is to get out the little snips and carefully trim it, or perhaps, if you're really smart, getting one of those hooked needle things to knit it back into the jumper. Alas, I was not the kind of capable person who carries little snips in their bag and as for being crafty, no, I was not.

Where were we? Oh yes, the loose thread. I suppose the

devil got into me because instead of doing a hundred other, better things, I reached down to that tiny, almost imperceptible, loose thread and tugged it, thinking it would snap. Yes, yes, you know it – instead of breaking, the thread held strong, and it was the seam that started to come apart. I didn't realise it at the time, but that was the beginning.

The train lurched to a stop and after a short, dark delay the driver's voice announced a signal failure would be keeping us here for a few minutes. A few turned into a full half hour and when I was eventually disgorged into the weak daylight, I was running five minutes late for the Monday morning all-hands standup on the tenth floor. While alone in the lift contemplating the horror of sidling into the meeting room, I couldn't resist giving that loose thread another tug and, predictably, another bit of seam gave way.

The lift came to a stop, but the doors didn't open. It took me more than a moment to realise I was stuck. I pushed the emergency button and, sounding very far away, an alarm began to ring. What would you think if it had happened to you? First the tube and now the lift, everything was going wrong. I was in a complete flap; I had no time to ponder the implications of my actions. Maybe you'd be quicker to put together cause and effect, but I doubt it. I think it is safe to say that the proverbial butterfly never understands the power of its wings.

Anyway, back in the present moment, I was cursing my bad luck and feeling very anxious about how to explain why I was so late because five minutes had turned into fifty by the time I finally made it into the office.

I get it, maybe you've only ever worked at places that are compassionate and understanding, but my manager at the time was neither of those things and to him to be on time was to already be late. He liked people to be at their desks early and stay late – this showed commitment and drive. I developed a serious Candy Crush habit in that job. My heart was pounding fit to burst and my palms were slick with sweat as late, dishevelled, I walked down the long rows of desks towards my own.

I never used to shut down. Sure, it trashes the laptop battery, but who cares when it gives you a few extra seconds of being online in the morning, possibly a whole minute, and saves you a few seconds at the end of the day when you want to head for the hills? I moved my mouse, autopilot typed this month's password from the post-it note on my monitor, and waited for Outlook to tell me what tedium awaited me.

My lateness passed unremarked, and complacency settled over my lap like a grandma-crocheted blanket. Now that I was safely where I was supposed to be, time was flowing like a swamp of molasses. Emails, spreadsheets, data entry. Finally, it was midday, time to break out the tub of leftover pasta and gulp it down al desko. I was crushing the candy, but still the loose thread tickled. Not physically, but it gave me a mental itch, an urge. Only willing to be partially reckless, holding the seam above to prevent further damage, I gave it another sharp yank. The thread pulled longer. The hole was noticeable and, beyond the seam, a row of knit now had a pull in it.

The meeting invite landed in my inbox like one of those blocks of blue ice frozen sewage that sometimes fall from planes – deadly if you're under it, but unnoticed by anyone else. Outlook's default setting is 30 minutes. It takes conscious effort to cut that back to a 15-minute slot.

So, obviously, after accepting the meeting requested by my manager, I took the precaution of testing the 'reply to all attendees' function. Fuck my life. He'd invited Guillo-Tina from people and culture. This was very definitely a bad news bears conversation.

The clock ticked. The sweat prickled. My skin itched. The afternoon dragged its feet like a waltz danced in chains – slow, slow, fucking hell quick. Finally, far too soon, it was time.

I opened the meeting room door to see Guillo-Tina smile in my direction like a hungry shark scenting blood.

Nerves? Of course I was nervous! I remember playing with my cuffs, tugging my hem.

I sat down and the meeting rolled over my head like a high tide. My tardiness, my lack of commitment, my crushing inability to perform.

My fingers found the forbidden thread and curled round it. I tugged. I pulled.

The meeting ended with me out of a job and seen to not just the lift, but the front door. My misconduct considered gross. A box would be couriered to my flat share, apparently.

In the company-paid-for cab, instead of assessing the ruin of my so-called career, I surveyed my own person. My jumper was now beyond subtly faulty. The seam gaped and there were missing stitches, entire empty rows, snaking across my stomach.

A strange energy filled me. Having passively watched the day's destruction, instead of trying to hold on to what remained, I was curious to see what else would and could break. Honestly? What's the worst that could happen?

We'd been together five years plus change. Since meeting

in freshers' week, Ed and I had been a thing, not a couple as such, more a conglomeration. We'd moved together from halls, to share house, to flat – motivated by comfort rather than desire.

I stomped into the tiled entryway of the house, slammed the door of the basement flat behind me, but the echo of my own actions was the only reply to greet me. Evidently Ed was still out.

Heating a tin of soup. Have you ever known such a thing for pathos? The sad turning of the can opener, the unappetising plop of the contents into a milk pan on a single burner (and that so much better than the cold, solitary bowl turning in a microwave that will create spots hotter than the sun while leaving oceans colder than the lunar landscape). That's where I was, trying to create sustenance from unpromising ingredients, when I heard Ed's heavy tread clump down the stairs, his key turn in the lock.

We exchanged the usual pleasantries. How are you? How was your day? Ed took up space. How had I never noticed this before? The oxygen for me to talk left the room, like a balloon untied after a party – there was no sudden bang just a long slow and sad fart of deflation.

While he told me about how he'd bested Jack from accounts with an excel of glory, I managed in my tugging to dislodge a single strand of yarn from my cuff. My fingernail caught on it, and then, worrying at it, I got a hold between fingertips.

What would you do? Snips? Hook needle thing? Take it off and donate it?

I held fast and I pulled at it. I pulled hard and sharp.

The loose thread held, and the sleeve started to unravel.

I like to think it was here, as Ed began to rant at me about my shortcomings, that I finally understood I had my own magic to thank for this destruction. However, if I'm honest, I still hadn't quite put the two-ply together.

After a lot of shouting, Ed left and slammed not just our door, but also the street door behind him. I was surprised, tragedy turned to comedy as he stomped up the steep flight of stairs. The cream of tomato had barely reached a simmer in the intervening time.

Tinned tomato soup's great, right? Delicious. The salty artificial gloopy tangy sweet, the soft pillowy bread, the hard, slippy, salty fat of the butter. I sat on the sofa alone and surveyed the day and, as I ate, I slurped.

What a ruin.

And then there was my jumper. Unravelled, coming apart at the seams – a perfect metaphor for how something so perfectly knitted together could disintegrate at the merest touch.

I put my tray with its crumbs and empty bowl – yes, I had my TV dinners on the sofa and on a tray, what of it? – on the ground. I took off my jumper and held it in my hands. I found a loose thread, by now there were several, and, considering, pulled.

The world continued to turn on its axis. The television blared.

Feeling stupid, and a little colder than comfortable, I put the jumper back on. But by now, looking at it, all I could see was fraying threads. The joy, the determination of demolition filled me. Destruction for its own sake. Destruction as an act of compassion, cruelty as necessity.

Both hands. Use both hands to do what's needed.

My fingers laced through the loose threads, round my ribs, towards my heart and other organs. Tangled in through the webbed holes of the knit, my fingers each snagged and curled inward. I held there for a moment, unsure if I really wanted to test the idea. Was I really ready to rip the very fabric of my being apart? Was I prepared to be disappointed when all that was left was two halves of a cheap sweater?

I clenched. I stretched my fists apart like a cheap Hulk. The fabric gave way.

The next few hours don't really bear the retelling. Needless to say, everything that I had assumed was close-knit in my family turned out to be rather shabby and frayed.

The day replayed itself across the cinema screen of my mind for days before I began to see the interconnection between my power and the outcome. Cause and effect – I do wonder, still, which way round it really is.

I enrolled in an evening class – stitch and bitch, knitting for beginners – and as my projects (a scarf, a pair of socks) slowly reached completion my life began to come back together too.

Not a witch? Fair comment. Magic isn't magic if you understand how it's done.

Hey, there's a thread hanging from your hem, let me…

Lisa Westhaven

From Switzerland to Melbourne - an unconventional love story

Leaving the snow-capped alps of Switzerland for the sunburnt shores of Melbourne, Australia was a dream of mine since I was a teenager. From my town where so many Swiss families or single adventurers had that strong longing to go to this land so far away.

So, my plan was, once I had finished school and all my necessary education, I would fulfil my dream.

My dear parents always knew I was a young lady full of longing for travel adventures and experiences. I'd lived and worked in a few countries and I truly loved those memories. My favourite experience was the opportunity in my early twenties to work in South Africa and Namibia. It was so exotic and different that I didn't want to come home to Switzerland. But the visa was unfortunately up and I had to go home.

Back home I became very restless and I made my decision to go to Australia. I had a contact in Melbourne which helped a lot. My parents were fine with the idea that I'd be away in a distant country for six months. My original plan was after my six months in Australia I would return to Switzerland to work in Geneva in a five-star hotel. As I could speak French and Italian, as well as my native Swiss German, there were lots of work opportunities back home with these languages in my skill set.

Geneva is a beautiful city - I visited there many times

when I was studying French in nearby Lausanne. It's very international and not as conservative as the German-speaking area of Switzerland I grew up in. Anybody who's been to the German-speaking part of Switzerland would know exactly what I am talking about.

I arrived in Melbourne - a city renowned for its vibrant culture and friendly people. I settled into my new surroundings straightaway - I felt like a local immediately. My first few weeks were spent exploring the city's sightseeing places. I was in awe of this amazing city.

One day, while strolling through a local market I struck up a conversation with a charming older women called Margaret. We bonded over our mutual love for fresh produce and cooking and she invited me over for afternoon tea the following week. I accepted the invitation, excited for the opportunity to experience a traditional Australian home.

Margaret's hospitality was evident from the moment I stepped into her home. As we sipped on tea and enjoyed homemade scones, we talked about everything from family to travel. She shared stories of her own adventures, and I shared mine. We formed a deep connection. And over the next few weeks, Margaret became like a second mother to me.

One evening as I was helping her prepare dinner, she casually mentioned that her son Patrick would be joining us for dinner. I had heard about her son Patrick a few times, but I hadn't given much thought to meeting him. However, when he walked through the door I was taken aback. He was charming and witty just like his mother and his demeanour made me feel instantly comfortable.

Dinner that night was filled with laughter and stories and I found myself drawn to Patrick in a way I hadn't expected. Over the next few weeks, Patrick and I began spending more time together. We discovered a shared love for hiking and our weekends were often spent exploring the stunning landscape around Melbourne. As our friendship deepened, so did our feelings for each other. It wasn't long before we realised that we were falling in love. Our relationship blossomed naturally and we became inseparable.

My parents were very happy for me - they could tell from my voice that I was blissfully in love.

Our wedding was a lovely intimate affair and everybody had a great time. It had a touch of Swiss culture – which meant some fun wedding games - and the Australian guests loved it. Something they had never seen before.

Looking back, my journey from Switzerland to Melbourne was more than just a travel adventure, it was a journey of the heart. Meeting my mother-in-law before meeting my husband was definitely unconventional, but it was the perfect start to our unique love story.

My parents gave me their blessing - and they also fell in love with this beautiful city.

I am so grateful for the wonderful life I have here in Melbourne.

Monika Nuesch

Perception

We've often said, haven't we,
he's a successful man
A dutiful son
loving husband
adoring father,
and quickly climbing the corporate ladder as well
Some clichés neatly fit

Why, wasn't it only the other day we said
with only a tinge of jealousy,
he seems to be travelling an interesting path
and, unlike most of us,
he has it all

and yes, we've often said
he can be distant at times
or wildly eccentric
and funny enough to be entertaining
when needed,
His success allows it

how then will we collect our thoughts
and reconcile the difference
between perception and reality,
when he is found next week
at still water's edge,
chiffon frills at bruised neck,
cherry red lipstick on dead mouth.

Sandra Lanteri

Endless blue

There was a day, spring 1994 when I was not yet 50, remembered vividly, food for musings; a glimpse of infinity.

Tacky. Hot. Under foot. All around. Above. Everywhere. Pungent. Blue.

And me at the deep end with walls surrounding.

Brush in hand, contemplating the transformation to my pool - recently emptied of water, its smooth concrete surface freshly painted with two coats of vivid aqua, reflecting a bizarre blue heat, indeed an unearthly place - a moving speck caught my eye. Puzzled I followed its motion for a while, then realising what it was, I watched captivated as it climbed and fell and climbed and fell.

"Darling, come look," I called out; he, working at the shallow end engrossed in paint and the footy blaring over the transistor radio, called back.

"What now, wife?"

"Come look," I insisted.

Grumbling a bit, careful to tread on dried sections painted the day before, he came. Seeing the speck, he made to crush it; just before contact he winked at me and stood by my side to watch this tiny thing, its body the size of a pinhead, eight legs barely visible, take tentative steps up the formidable vertical side of the pool, slipping every few centimetres, fall towards the bottom, struggle up again, a manifestation of an exercise in futility; Sisyphus sans myth-saga, sans a stone[1].

"Imagine," I said,
"Imagine what the world looks like to this baby spider: sheer surface, sticky, hot; endless blue."

He checked out the pool and sky, nodded, smiled. I picked up a fallen gum leaf and scooping the little spider onto the leaf, I reached up on tiptoes, placed it carefully in the cool green grass of the verge; back to work we went: wielding paintbrushes, applying the third coat of blue, relishing the spring sun.

As I worked, I contemplated the spider's miraculous survival.

Just days ago, I had removed remnants of the gossamer-fine sticky bubbles of egg-filled sacs from under the projecting lip of the brick pool edge, which, chosen by eager spider-mothers-to-be as a safe place, proved to be a very poor choice; this attested to by the hatchlings aplenty that, fallen to watery death, had clouded the pool surface.

I suppose this tiny one emerged late, after the pool was emptied, from a fragment of sac that I'd missed. Having survived death by drowning or crushing, it had fallen the more than two metres to the pool bottom; intact, driven by an instinct to climb, though with no concept of to what and where, it had begun its life-journey climbing upwards and, if not rescued, would have died knowing only slippery blue and glaring heat. I wondered,

> "What do you, little spider, make of the world?"
>> There and then a realisation struck, an epiphany, insight to a question universal.
>>> Was not this spider's experience of the all-surrounding blue
>>>> an analogy for Man's perception
>>>>> of his world?

***

Years have rolled by in my life, and, to appease the hunger for an answer, I watch and read everything I can that offers an insight into the universe.

I have learnt that the beautiful webs spiders spin and construct are themselves known as *approximate finite fractals*[2], a concept far beyond spider contemplation. In their endless patterns, *self-similar fractals* are simultaneously complex and familiar. These fractals, visible to us through multitudinous aspects of nature such as trees, rivers, coastlines, mountains, clouds, seashells, hurricanes, demonstrate both chaos and order. *Abstract fractals* exemplified by the *Mandelbrot Set*[3], generated by a computer calculating a simple equation over and over, beautiful and terrifying in their variety, repetition, and sometimes bizarre forms, offer a glimpse of the infinite. Parallel to these esoteric concepts, current theories to explain the observed and imagined universe are testing; these postulate ten dimensions, or more, to enchant and bewilder.

Most of us comprehend the dimensions as three: one's a line, two makes a plane, three creates volume; add time and we have the fourth dimension where science and imagination collide.[4]

After that, attune your mind to the likes of quantum and other physics to comprehend these unknowables. Or, watch *Dr Who*[5]. Check out the five to ten online and discover the extraordinary: there are any number of possible futures, the single outcome we experience is an act of choice, the fifth and sixth dimensions are the branching of each possible future, mastery of these dimensions could enable time-travel; the dimensions seven through ten deal with universes that each have their own progressions of dimensional reality and possible outcomes.[6] All this substantiated by important scientists including the likes of Stephen Hawking and Paul Davies.

My imagination leaps from blackboards dense with symbols beyond my ken to the sight and sound of the TARDIS[7] careening through space. It seems the familiar stuff of sci-fi is indeed exploring the conundrums of the dimensions of modern science!

Back in time to the spring day of 1994.

Yes, I thought, we see, measure, imagine; ultimately, are we, like the tiny spider in the pool, unable to comprehend even a minute fraction of the majesty and mystery of the whole of creation? Perhaps, I mused, perhaps, like Twilight-Zone-fancying, our whole universe is but a speck in some other being's world – say, a molecule of paint or a spiderling trapped in an empty pool?

I laughed at the imagery and thought: Have a good life, little spider.

A roar emanated from the tranny; game over. We won! Yea!

"Time for a cuppa?" I called to my man.

"I'll have a beer, thanks," was his reply.

I climbed out of that empty pool.
All was green, verdant, fragrant in my garden.
What a relief to exit the endless blue.

Endnotes

1 http://en.wikipedia.org/wiki/Sisyphus accessed 24 September 2014

2 http://en.wikipedia.org/wiki/Fractal accessed 24 September 2014

3 Cyberwatch - Masterpiece: Colours of Infinity (UK) 11 November 1996 on SBS TV.

4 https://science.howstuffworks.com/science-vs-myth/everyday-myths/see-the-fourth-dimension.htm accessed 15/5/2024

5 http://www.doctorwhotv.co.uk/ accessed 24 September 2014

6 http://www.universetoday.com/48619/10-dimensions/ accessed 23 September 2014

7 Dr Who's time machine and spaceship – bigger on the inside. TARDIS = Time And Relative Dimension in Space http://www.thedoctorwhosite.co.uk/tardis/ Accessed 24 September 2014

Sara Vidal

Unbreakable

Sticks and stones beating upon multiple bones.
Tearing at my flesh.
Bruising my brain.
My unbreakable bones.
My impermeable skin.
My fortressed mind.
Have back your sticks.
Have back your stones.
I have placed them in a pile for you.
Your words no longer penetrate me.

Jennifer Baker

The etiquette conundrum:
Bringing manners back – or at least tryingto

So, here's the thing – manners. What happened to them? We used to have them, right? People said "please," they said "thank you," they held the door open. Now? Now it's like everyone's in their own little world, and nobody cares. You're lucky if you get a grunt of acknowledgment. What's going on?

The vanishing act of common courtesy

Sixty years ago, you'd see a guy walking down the street, and he'd tip his hat. Tipping a hat! Can you imagine someone doing that today? They'd probably throw out their neck. But it was a thing – people were polite. You didn't just walk past someone without a nod, a wave, something! Fast forward to now, and we're living in a world where the best you can hope for is someone not stepping on your toes as they cut in line.

Take the elevator, for example. Back then, you stepped inside, made eye contact, maybe even struck up a little conversation. Now? You're lucky if anyone even acknowledges your existence. It's like riding in a silent tube of awkwardness. And when did people stop saying "excuse me"? They just push past you like you're a piece of furniture that's inconveniently placed. What are we, invisible?

And what about crossing the street? There used to be a

whole dance of eye contact and hand waves – "You go, no, you go!" Now, it's a game of chicken. Is anyone slowing down? Is that car going to stop? It's a gamble every time you leave the curb.

The digital wild west
Let's talk about digital manners. Or should I say, the complete and utter lack of them? Remember when answering the phone was an event? You picked it up, you said, "Hello, how are you?" You might even chat for a minute, ask about the family. Now it's all texts and emails. "Thx" and "u there?" Where's the respect? We've reduced human interaction to acronyms! Who's got the time for real words anymore?

And don't even get me started on social media. It's a free-for-all out there! People say things online they'd never say to your face. No filter, no boundaries. Everyone has an opinion, generally spiced with emotion designed to disturb. And don't you dare disagree – suddenly you're in a full-blown digital duel. It's like the Wild West, but instead of guns, people are using memes and snarky comments. "I'll see you at high noon, and I'll bring my gif game!"

And the oversharing – oh, the oversharing! Do I need to know what you had for breakfast? Do I really care that you're "so over it today"? People are airing their dirty laundry like it's prime-time TV. What happened to a little mystery, a little decorum?

The mysterious case of the missing "Thank You"
Remember when you did something nice, and you'd get a thank you? I miss those days. You'd hold the elevator, and someone would say, "Thank you, good sir!" Well, maybe not exactly like that, but you get the idea. Now, you hold the elevator, and they walk in like you're their personal

doorman. No nod, no smile, nothing. It's like you're part of the architecture, just there to serve.

We're living in a time where the bar for gratitude is so low, it's practically underground. What happened to "please" and "thank you"? These are basic words, people! I'm not asking for a sonnet; just a little acknowledgment.

And what's with the disappearing act of handwritten thank-you notes? Remember those? You'd get a gift, and you'd sit down with a pen and some nice stationery, and you'd write a thank you note. Now, you're lucky if you get a "thx" text, if that. People act like writing a note is akin to climbing Everest. "Oh, I'll just send a quick text." Quick? Quick is the problem! We've turned something meaningful into a task to be checked off a list.

The workplace: A manners-free zone?

And let's not forget the workplace. The office used to be a place of decorum, a little slice of civility. Now, it's like a jungle. People are yelling across cubicles, eating tuna fish at their desks (tuna fish!), and nobody's holding the door for anybody. It's every man for himself.

Remember when meetings were formal? You showed up on time, you were prepared, and you paid attention. Now, people are waltzing in late, plopping down with their soy coffee like they're at a café, and half the room is checking their phones under the table. And the multitasking – oh, the multitasking! People are typing away on laptops during meetings, not paying attention at all. "Oh, sorry, what was that? I was just answering an email." No, you were ignoring the meeting. Let's call it what it is.

We've got a new generation in the workplace, and they've brought their casual, "whatever" attitude with them. Jeans to a meeting? Sure, why not? We're all equals here, right?

It's all about comfort. Well, what about the comfort of not seeing your boss's toes in flip-flops during a presentation? Ever think of that?

And when did the office kitchen become a battleground? There's food theft, passive-aggressive notes, and don't even get me started on the microwave situation. You'd think people were raised in a barn the way they leave messes behind. "Oh, I'll just leave my exploded spaghetti sauce here. Someone will clean it up." Yeah, someone – like a cleaning fairy that doesn't exist.

The dinner table debacle

Speaking of comfort, let's talk about dining. Remember when eating was an event? You'd sit at the table, use utensils, maybe even have a conversation. Now, everyone's eating in front of the TV, or worse, the computer. Elbows on the table? Sure, who cares? Chewing with your mouth open? Why not, it's just me and Netflix.

And don't get me started on phones at the table. Who decided it was okay to scroll through Instagram while someone's trying to tell you about their day? It's like we've all forgotten how to eat like civilized human beings. You want to eat on the couch? Fine. But can we at least agree to chew with our mouths closed?

Remember the days when dinner was a social occasion? You'd talk, you'd laugh, maybe argue a little, but it was all part of the experience. Now, everyone's so engrossed in their screens, you're lucky if you get a grunt between bites. "How was your day?" *Grunt.* "Anything new at work?" *Grunt.* It's like living with a pack of distracted wolves.

And what's with the portion sizes? It's like people are eating for a family of four, by themselves. When did we decide that bigger is better? A plate should not be the size of a small car tyre. And don't even get me started on the art of conversation. We've lost it, people. We've traded witty banter for emoji-laden text speak. It's a tragedy.

The casual conundrum
Then there's this whole thing with dress codes. Sixty years ago, people dressed up for everything. Flying on a plane? You wore a suit. Going to the theatre? Out comes the fancy dress. Today, people are showing up to weddings in flip-flops. Flip-flops! It's like everyone's decided that comfort trumps decorum.

And look, I'm all for being comfortable. But there's a time and a place. Wearing sweatpants to a nice restaurant? That's not comfort – that's giving up. We've gone from dressing to impress to dressing like we're heading to the gym. Can we bring back just a little effort?

The "casualization" of society has reached new lows. Remember when you'd get dressed up just to go out for a coffee? Now, people are rolling out of bed and heading straight to the regular coffee shop in their pyjamas. Pyjamas! In public! What are we, sleepwalking through life? We've gone from suits and ties to sweatpants and flip-flops, and it's not an upgrade.

And weddings – oh, don't get me started on weddings. There was a time when people understood that a wedding was a special occasion. You dressed up. You looked nice. Now, you've got people showing up in jeans and T-shirts. To a wedding! It's like they're saying, "Sure, I'll come to your special day, but I'm not going to put in any effort." We've gone from black-tie to no-tie, and it's a slippery slope.

Can we fix this?

So, how do we fix this? How do we bring back the manners, the respect, the good old-fashioned courtesy? It's like trying to put toothpaste back in the tube – it's not going to be easy.

First off, we've got to start with ourselves. Be the change, right? Hold the door, say "thank you," put the phone down when someone's talking to you. It's not that hard; it's just basic courtesy for our fellow human.

And let's talk about kids. What happened to teaching kid's manners? You know, before they become little phone-obsessed robots. We've got to start early – show them how to write a thank you note, how to shake a hand (not too hard, not too soft), and how to look someone in the eye when they're talking. These are skills, people, and they're disappearing faster than a plate of shrimp at a buffet.

It's time to bring back etiquette classes. You know, the ones where you learned which fork to use, how to introduce people, and, most importantly, how to be a decent human being. Imagine that – etiquette classes making a comeback. It's like bringing back the dodo bird, but more important.

And what about the digital world? It's time for some etiquette. No more all-caps yelling, no more trolling. Just a little respect for the other human on the other side of the screen. Maybe we need a course, something like "Internet Manners 101." I'd take it!

We need to teach people that there's a person on the other side of that tweet or comment. It's not just a username; it's a real live person. Maybe we could implement some kind of online courtesy meter – every time you say something nice, you get points. Say something rude? You lose points. It's like a video game, but for decency.

The bottom line

In the end, it's all about respect. Manners aren't just about following rules; they're about making the world a little less annoying. So, let's bring them back. Because let's face it, the world could use a little more "please" and a little less "meh." We've done worse things – we brought back vinyl records, so why not manners?

And who knows? Maybe, just maybe, we can make tipping a hat cool again. Okay, probably not. But it's worth a shot, right?

At the very least, we can start with the basics – holding doors, saying "thank you," and putting the phone down during dinner. It's not much, but it's a start. And if we all make a little effort, maybe we can turn this ship around. Or at least make it a little less likely that we'll get a door slammed in our face.

After all, wouldn't it be nice to live in a world where people say "please" and "thank you," where they hold doors, and where the most controversial thing online is a debate about the best pizza toppings? It's a dream, sure, but it's one worth chasing. So, let's give it a shot.

Ed Davis

The 'A' word

"Is that you, David?' Faith called from the kitchen. 'Dinner's ready'.

She'd spent much of the afternoon preparing the food – roast beef and vegetables accompanied by Yorkshire pudding – David's favourite. The apple pie was in the oven .

David took a bottle of wine from the refrigerator, a glass from the kitchen cupboard, then sat down. No point in asking Faith if she would like a drink, she would say 'no,' like she always did. What he would like was for her to join him in a glass of wine before dinner. But her head was full of that religious stuff - no drinking, no dancing, nothing to brighten up their lives. She wouldn't even come to the pub for dinner, like other doctor's wives. Why, he couldn't fathom. Was it the hotel food or was it that she was dead against pubs and all they represented.

Faith served the dinner. David noticed the small amount of food on his wife's plate, but decided not to say anything. He'd tried it before, but it hadn't worked.

Faith cut her food into tiny pieces, then using a fork to bring each   morsel to her mouth, began to masticate the food, slowly and painfully.

David watching, could stand it no longer. 'For God's sake, Faith, eat up the stuff otherwise there'll be nothing left of you.'

'I'm doing my best,' Faith said, with tears in her eyes.

She removed the plates and took them to the kitchen.

'Like some apple pie?'

David said 'yes.' He was feeling bad at having criticized his wife. The truth was he was concerned about her health and didn't know what to do about it.

When Faith retired for the night, David poured himself another drink. He felt empty. Was it because Faith had been unable to give him the child he wanted or was it that she no longer attracted him. All he knew was that he was bored with the way things were. He wanted some fun and laughter, a spark in his life. He resolved to take up bushwalking. Anything to get him out of the house.

Faith undressed, slipped on her nightgown then knelt down beside the bed to pray. She prayed for the sick, for the needy, for those serving on the mission fields, the elderly, the poor, the sad, the lonely. Satisfied she had covered the whole gamut of misery, she got into bed and reached for the bible. After reading a chapter from the Ephesians, she put out the light.

As she lay there, her eyes wide open, she thought that she had never felt so unhappy. And yet – she had everything, a loving husband, a comfortable home and a bounteous garden. She burst into tears. It's all my fault, she thought. It's all my fault.

Lorraine Doney

The exhibition

Georgie was frantic. Her day in the sun had arrived. Mr Edwards, the owner of the prestigious gallery where she worked, was very protective of his stellar reputation. He had struggled to relinquish any creative control. She'd been working there for over a year and, thus far, her job had consisted of mainly administrative tasks like banking, producing catalogues, organising the catering, issuing invitations and co-ordinating pick-ups and deliveries. Georgie took great care not to make any mistakes. Mr Edwards was a perfectionist. He didn't tolerate mistakes.

Melbourne was considered by many (Melburnians) to be the cultural capital of Australia. The National Gallery of Victoria was renowned for its wonderful permanent collection of famous local artists from the nineteenth century like Arthur Streeton and Hans Heyson, as well as a magnificent collection of works by indigenous artists. In addition, there was a superb collection of European Masters from ancient civilizations through to the popular expressionist collection as well as many popular contemporary artists. Mr Edward's Gallery was at, what the locals call, *the Paris end of Collins Street* in the CBD. It was nestled among some of the finest heritage buildings and theatres, was near to the seat of the State Government, and the upmarket retail outlets of the fashion houses of Europe.

It had been Georgie's dream job after she had qualified. But, like most aspiring careers, the anticipation of its potential was overshadowed by the mundanity of its reality. It was a lonely job most of the time, as the gallery wasn't busy unless there was an opening. So, considering all this, for Mr Edwards, seemingly out of the blue, to suggest that she curate the upcoming Max Pointer exhibition had rendered Georgie momentarily speechless. Nevertheless, suggest it he had, and as Max Pointer was something of a drawcard, it was even more remarkable. Max had recently had a series of very successful exhibitions around the country and had featured on a highly regarded art programme on the national broadcaster. He'd also won an important national art prize. Max Pointer was known to be very hands on with the installations, so Georgie could only assume that Mr Edwards had reasoned that she wouldn't mess it up.

Today, Monday, the artworks were being delivered and Max's manager, Leslie, had suggested that she allow three or four days to set up the installation. The opening would take place this upcoming Saturday. All the invitations had been dispatched and, judging from the number of acceptances so far, it would be a packed house.

Georgie arrived at the gallery at 6:00am on Monday morning. It was still quite dark outside, even though it was the tail end of summer. The truck was due to arrive at 7:00am and she wanted to make sure the four main rooms, and vast hallway interconnecting them, were spick and span ready to receive the valuable artwork. She swept and mopped the already mopped floors and polished all the window ledges, gave all the windows a once over and checked that all the lighting was working. She had the electrician on standby in case she needed to adjust or add anything. At 8:15am the truck arrived, and Georgie guided it into the loading space at the rear of the gallery, not a little shocked at the size of the vehicle. Two men jumped out and stood looking expectantly at her.

'Did Leslie not give you a document to hand to me on arrival?'

'No Miss; nothing.'

Well maybe Leslie was on his way with the installation notes now.

'Ok, well we'd better unload; we are blocking the entrance to the back lane.'

This was always a drama as all the businesses on that block shared the same back lane access. Georgie wondered if the removal men had any idea of the value contained within.

A collection of objects put together by a creative genius to demonstrate humanity's reluctance to embrace the simple truths of its existence; to send a powerful message to the viewers (and art collectors).

To slough off the meaningless trappings of our consumerism and become more attuned to nature and each other.'

The theme of this current exhibition.

Well, that's what Georgie had read in the blurb anyway. She was excited to finally meet Max Pointer. He was notoriously reclusive, there were no photographs of him online and apparently, he disliked crowds, often lurking behind curtains during an opening. Naturally this quirky behaviour had endeared him to the enthusiastic art collectors among us, propelling Max's popularity into the stratosphere and accounting for the exorbitant pricing of his work.

The catalogue Georgie had produced (from the garbled information Leslie had sent) was a complex chronicle of sorts. Rather than an itemized list of artworks along with their pricing, it was more like a set of descriptive journal entries with price suggestions at the end. This was most unusual and encouraged a bidding frenzy at every opening.

It was a marketing trick which convinced people that they might miss out on a potentially lucrative opportunity. Known more succinctly as FOMO. Hence, the prices just got higher and higher as people competed for the works.

Max Pointer's installations were not in the least bit conventional, they consisted of sculptural and domestic items curated together in such a way so that they told a story. It was up to the imagination of the viewer to discern the message from the scant information Max provided. For example, he once paired a beautiful Venetian face mask, decorated with meticulously hand painted artwork and hand-woven lace studded with semi-precious stones, with a blow-up life size doll. The story behind this 'creation', designed to portray the primal, licentious nature of men and their desperate attempts to hide it beneath a superficial veneer or personality; disguised as something attractive but which has no real substance. It resonated with an American collector who paid over a million dollars for it. Pure madness, thought Georgie, or pure genius? Who was she to say?

In the meantime, she was trying to get hold of Leslie, but the phone kept going straight to voicemail. She didn't have Max's mobile phone number.

She was just going to have to use her limited knowledge of Max's style and attempt to assemble the collection herself. Surely the items would be labelled and packed accordingly, she wasn't too concerned.

When the truck doors were opened, she observed, thankfully, that the contents were arranged in neat bundles, or in boxes. Unfortunately, none of the bundles or boxes were labelled. However, she had the catalogue in front of her containing the title of each artwork and assumed (and prayed) she would be able to identify each set of items from that.

She directed the men, and the cargo was promptly rehoused. Georgie randomly allocated the mix of bundles and boxes to the four main rooms, spreading them out allowing enough space to walk around each installation so the visitors could comfortably observe the genius on display.

Ok, One bundle at a time. The first one she tackled consisted of a set of random books, novels, art history, biographies, art books, crime thrillers, and a complete set of the works of Beatrice Potter. Right, so this must be the domestic component she reasoned. Then along with these was a beautiful antique silver cutlery set, all pieces accounted for, arranged in specifically sized sections in a walnut box with royal blue velvet lining. It was divine. That's domestic too, she thought. In addition, there were a few different board games including a scrappy looking Guess Who? a scrabble, a casino set (which contained a roulette wheel with counters and a roll out table mat of the numbers), a boggle, a very classy chess set and several packs of cards including Uno. The final item was a shoebox. She opened it to discover a miniature world. A tiny little hand painted porcelain tea set, three little crystal animals, a pig, a unicorn and a squirrel. A miniature Miss Piggy and a miniature Kermit. A fairy house made from some kind of resin with sparkles all over it. A pair of miniature Dutch clogs and a set of black castanets (normal size). *Right! Time to scour the catalogue and make sense out of this installation.* After reading through several titles, she came across; "The Myth of childhood." The blurb then went on to say, 'the blatant fabrications and deceptions we perpetrate on our young and the harm it inflicts.'

That must be it! Max would inform on a verbal basis if asked to give a fuller explanation behind his reasoning, but he wanted the observers to work it out for themselves. Therefore, no more was written on the catalogue. His exhibitions often generated a lot of conversation, and much controversy, as to the rationale behind each work of art. Georgie supposed it was a good idea to encourage the dialogue in such a way as people generally inspired and encouraged each other (to purchase). Looking at this exhibit, Georgie tried to decipher the meaning behind it.

The miniature playthings and fantasy books from childhood pointing to the innocence with which we are all born. A unicorn, representing that thing which is most pure and without guile. Then the board games encouraging competition and deception, calculation and cunning. Stripping away the virtue one game at a time. Culminating in knowledge (think Adam and Eve) represented by the adult book collection, including therein the horrors perpetrated by man on his own kind (crime) and finally, possessions of monetary value, (the silver cutlery set) pointing to the carnal sin of avarice. An exposé of our moral decline.

Pleased that she had figured out this first one, she began working on its arrangement. She decided to layer it using shelves of decreasing heights. She reasoned the childhood items should be placed in a bright spotlight at the top with the unicorn first and centre. And then using the suggestion of age progression, placing the games lower down in a more subtle light with the books and finally the cutlery at the base in comparative darkness; maybe even with a reddish hue suggesting a darkness; as in hell. *Ha! What a brilliant idea!* When she had finished, it looked fantastic.

And so, the next few days continued in this way as Georgie

painstakingly analysed each installation from the only thing she had, the titles in the catalogue. Some were quite simple but there were a couple she was worried about. The box that gave her most grief contained a set of spanners, an angle grinder, some ropes and extension cords-along with some blankets, cushions and two matching lamps. One of the lamps was missing its shade which was the only clue she could fathom to meet the title's brief.

'A Dark Heart in Shade.' Very sinister, but then a lot of his work was. She couldn't quite fathom its full meaning.

The opening night was upon her. Georgie hadn't slept a wink last night. The whole experience had been more stressful than it should. Mr Edwards had called Georgie late the first day to inform her that Max and Leslie had recently broken up and Max had moved out. She hadn't known prior to that but they had been live-in partners for decades. As a result, Max was too upset to come to the gallery. He wasn't even sure he'd be there on opening night. Leslie had apparently absconded to Spain with some stolen money and a young Irish boy called Fergus.

The show must go on. It was a resounding success. Even 'Dark Heart in Shade' had sold for hundreds of thousands of dollars. Georgie was so relieved, and Mr. Edwards was delighted. The exhibition ran for three weeks and visitors crowded the gallery most days. All the works had sold on the first night. Max didn't come to the opening, but Georgie had hinted he might be there to anyone who asked. It was just a little subterfuge and it certainly added to the intrigue and marketability of this reclusive artist.

All the installations were delivered to their happy clients.

The following week Georgie was working on the next

exhibition when Mr. Edwards came out of his office looking very pale.

"That was Max Pointer on the phone. He went to retrieve the contents of one of his storage units to move them into his new apartment. It was empty. Then he checked his adjacent one and found all his art installations still there."

Anna Auditore

Lost in transition

Nowhere is anywhere
anywhere is somewhere
somewhere is far away
far away is not far enough
everything is nothing
nothing is something

he can't remember
how long he's been on the road
but one day
he might get to where he's going
then he'll understand
why he started out
Or maybe not

Sandra Lanteri

Temptation

You debate, you bargain, you reason,
and come to the conclusion that you really don't want,
so, you rationalize some more
regardless of being in the moment

Despite all that thinking, all that thought
You know you're guilty and haven't bothered changing the score
all that is secondary
the turmoil of do or don't.

It's simply a religion of just give me more
And I'll change later.
You fall to your knees
And bow your head
Wanting forgiveness as you
fall into temptation again.

If this were medieval times,
where you probably didn't really repent,
your head would have been long gone.

Peter Levy

The day

I think I had a good day at school. I liked the book the teacher read us as we sat on the mat late in the afternoon. I liked the picture that I drew with the big crayons and I put it in my bag to take home and show Mum. I really liked playtime and the piece of cake that I had in my lunchbox. Every lunchtime after we had eaten, we had to go to the wash taps and wash our hands using the little container of soap that we all had. The soap was kept in our toilet bag. Mine was yellow with little flowers all over it.

My sister and I always walked home together. She was in grade five and often didn't want to play with me. I hated in when she pushed me away and told me I was a nuisance when I was near her friends. But every day she walked home with me, mainly because Mum had told her to. We often played that game of trying not to walk on the cracks in the pavement, in case the devil got you.

We always came home through the back door. We didn't have a key for the front door. Up the two steps, open the wire screen door, into the laundry part and then open the door to the kitchen. There was a step up into the kitchen. But that day the kitchen door was locked. It was never locked. We rattled the door handle, or at least my sister did, but it wouldn't open. There was a strong smell near the door. I knew it was gas, the gas smell that came from our cooker when the matches didn't light the gas.

I felt not right. Something was wrong, not just the locked

door. We yelled out for Mum but no answer came. I think we yelled out a lot, probably walking around to the front of the house. We had good friends who were neighbours around the corner. They lived on the corner of the next street and my sister and I somehow made our way around to their place. I don't remember the talk, what my sister must have said. But an underneath feeling of something bad was in my stomach.

I remember we sat down and ate biscuits and had cordial while my friend's mother did something. Ringing someone? Or walking around the block to our house? All I remember is we didn't go back home, we ended up at our Auntie Audrey's place. She lived two streets away and was my mum's sister. We would often walk around to their house to play with our cousins, sometimes after school and sometimes on the weekend.

All that time I felt not right, worried, scared and sure something had happened. Where was my mum?

I found out she was dead I think later that day, although it is all very hazy. Some of my memories are crystal clear sixty years later and others not so. Another aunt features prominently in memory.

I think it was the same day. I am standing near a telephone table in the entrance hall of my mother's sister's house.

The telephone is black Bakelite and the table has a little telephone Teledex, with all the letters of the alphabet down one side and a little lever to scroll down to the letter you wanted. This aunt is my father's sister and I am screaming at her, screaming with the grief and anger and despair of a six-year-old who wants her mother and intuitively knows she will not come back. We are the only people in that space, isolated away from the rest of the occupants. My aunt is holding my arms trying to stop my rage and yelling back at me, no doubt out of her depth and in the depths of her own despair and shock. I remember her being tall and strong, telling me to get a grip or words to that effect. How can you say that to a six -year- old?

I pity the role she had to play, not one of her choosing I imagine, one that my other aunt probably fobbed off to her. Perhaps my mum's sister was distraught. Perhaps she just didn't want to deal with the messiness of grief.

I am a handful. I cannot be placated, pacified or calmed. I think I sobbed and sobbed for days.

The days merged, we stayed with our cousins for some time, with everyone it seemed tiptoeing around us. I wanted to be home but home was never to be the same again.

She had chosen to put her head in the gas oven, an ugly green enamel affair and leave the gas running. Coal gas in those days was poisonous and I supposed she just went to sleep eventually suffocating with the fumes. I sometimes imagine the coldness of that oven door against her face.

That gas cooker remained in the kitchen, a constant macabre reminder of what had happened. We had no money to replace it.

Dianne Motton

365

The world feels heavy,
Like a storm that never ends,
Clouds thick with worry
And the weight of things
We cannot fix.
Everything seems to break
Under careless hands,
And the ground we stand on
Feels uncertain.
Yet somewhere,
A seed is still sprouting,
Pushing through the cracks,
Unseen but determined.
In the darkest moments,
A light persists,
Faint as a whisper
But present all the same.
People still reach
For one another,
Even when they stumble,
And the smallest acts of kindness
Reshape the world
In ways we'll never see.
Maybe we don't heal everything,
But hope isn't about the grand gestures—
It's the quiet belief
That tomorrow still holds something
Worth holding on to.

Amanda Divers

What helps people?

Apart from dance I suggest three little things, you choose of course
Pray for good things, give thanks for what is, and the ones that have helped
To put hands on their laps, to quiet and discipline the mind and watch the thoughts in their mind
From negative to positive and practice this
To quieten, discipline the mind and emotions and practice this
To use my hands for sculpting or pen to paper
With clay I sculpt, an earthy smooth feel, to sculpt an idea, to sculpt a head or torso, to sculpt a wave from the sea, for me and thee
To write poems and stories inspired by the world, by my imagination
The blue pen I use, a bit darker than the blue sky
We feel better when the sky is blue
Happens to be the color of Medicine Buddha, he's blue
A special color blue as Buddha was a special kind of man
There have been many masters, not all were men, all to help us in ways that would delight
They paved the way to guide us in their ways as that is the way
Messages to understand, to find ways to live again, ways to feel again, to live in this world that has become fragmented, quite strange at times.
So I remember there were ones that paved the way

Rose Lumbaca Crane

To my precious Mother

Oh, so soon you left me. I was not prepared for this sad moment, even though one day I knew I had to face losing you. I am in shock and feel so sad that I am not allowed to be there in these last moments of your life. I wish I could sit next to you holding your warm hands, looking at your loving, kind smile. But it wasn't meant to be.

But I am so grateful for all the caring people you have around you. They all love you – with great admiration.

You are a special Mother who brought sunshine into everyone's heart.

Your beautiful smile, your kindness and generosity will never be forgotten.

All my friends in Australia all adored you so much.

But we all know that you are in a better heavenly place now, surrounded by my kind Papa, your parents, your relatives and friends who have also left this earthly planet and are also with the heavenly father.

Your wonderful life will continue forever with our dear God and you will never be forgotten by your loved ones.

(The wooden bench I have memorized for you and Papa, will be there forever; and for everyone's enjoyment. It is always a good conversation to start with a stranger).

Dearest Mum I miss you so much, words cannot describe it and I know one day we will meet again.

Your loving daughter

Monika

Monika Nuesch

Whenever the table

Whenever the table's full,
    we pull up another table;
whenever the talking stops,
    we find another topic;
whenever the weather's bleak,
    we curl up on the couch
with a good book and a doona.

Whenever I see your face
    a smile invades my being
    and spreads from ear to ear,
    from head to toe,
    from here to here ;
    my inventive place,
    my infinite space.

Ann Simic

Stone soup (a German folk tale)

The lonely traveler could hardly see to make his way through the thick snow as he stumbled towards a small group of houses.

He looked forward to a hot meal and a warm place to sleep for the night. An old woman looked at him suspiciously as she opened the door of the house he came to.

"Can you give me a piece of bread; I am so hungry?"

She told him to go away for she had scarcely enough for herself.

At every door he knocked on, the answer was the same. No luck.

Pulling his thin overcoat over his thin shoulders he walked on until he came to a cooking pot that was filled with snow. Out of his pocket he took a smooth stone and threw it into the pot.

"This winter is so harsh, we can all do with a hearty meal", he said as he stirred the contents of the pot.

"What are you doing?" asked a little girl who was watching him with interest.

"I'm making stone soup," he replied, stirring the snow.

"If I get an onion to add to your soup, will you share it with me?" she asked.

"Certainly," said the man, smiling as though he knew what would happen next.

Sure enough, the old woman came out of her house

bringing some salt to add to the soup. One by one, people brought things to add; cabbage, carrot, a leek.

"If we bring our bits and pieces, will you share your soup with us?" they asked.

"Sure, sit down. There will be enough for everyone."

Soon they were all seated around a table sharing a hearty bowl of soup, and the fragrant aroma made them radiate with contentment for the first time in months. The little girl enjoyed the soup and asked the traveler if she could keep the stone. He looked and found it at the bottom of the pot, and then wiped it dry.

"Here you are," he said. "If you keep this with you always, you will never be hungry or lonely again".

The little girl loved the smooth round stone, because she knew it was indeed a treasure.

Dita Gould

Surrounded by others I feel alone

Surrounded by others I feel alone.
Talking out loud in monotone
Standing before you I feel unseen.
Scouring my flesh, yet still unclean.
Sobbing silently, no tears fall.
I open my heart, yet reveal nothing at all.
Moving lips, no words spill forth.
Peering inside, seeing no self worth.
Unworthy, unheard, unseen, unclean.
Alone, Invisible, silent, obscene.

Jennifer Baker

Power seizing fiasco - 1967

In early January, Inner Mongolia, we heard from the loudspeaker just outside our house that under Madam Mao's leadership, Shanghai Radicals had seized power from the establishment. Father said Chairman Mao sent a telegraph to support the Shanghai Radicals and described it just like Father had said: *it was one class overthrew another class. This was a great revolution. Learn from Shanghai!* By now, I had learned if it was revolution, it was good.

It was an icy January winter night, and the Gobi Desert wind was howling outside. Inside our house, the potbelly stove burned brightly, cosy and warm. Our large brick bed was crowded with about twenty people from the Radical Faction, and all gathered around Father who was at the bed table writing on Company letterhead paper. People talked; he wrote. I didn't know whether it was his extremely beautiful fountain pen characters or his little brush characters or that he wrote fantastic articles, but every time someone wanted something to be written in the company, Father was the person they called upon. I was so proud he was quite a power among the group.

The core members of the Radical Faction in the company gathered in our house, planning to seize power from the Conservatives, just like the Shanghai Rebels. Father's penmanship was used to write out the plan of the revolution.

Uncle Sun sat next to Father. He called Father an Ironpen. Uncle Sun was young and energetic. He'd become a telegram technician. He was tall and thin, with big eyes and fair skin. He talked loudly and laughed heartily. Most importantly, he came from a poor peasant background and had been in the army. Chairman Mao trusted people like him to carry out his revolution.

The Radical Faction appointed him as their chief, and he loved this new status. Father always said, 'His major handicap is lack of education, and he has to stop joking about.' But I liked him because he loved to tease Tiger and me. He was young and handsome and his beautiful wife was pregnant with her large belly carrying their first baby.

Tiger and I were squashed into a corner of the bed, listening.

One uncle said to the crowd, 'I will take the security manager and a few people to take over the directors' offices. I will lock away the official seals. You take more people and stop the Conservatives from coming near us.'

Then they discussed setting up a Revolutionary Committee. Father obtained a position as Chief Consultant and was heaped with honour. That made me happy too.

'I predict the Shanghai revolution is merely the beginning of power seizure. It will spread to the whole country. We must be well prepared for the day,' Father said.

Tiger and I lost interest because neither of us understood what they were talking about. Then Uncle Sun moved over to us. He asked in a low voice, 'Would you like to hear a story?'

'Yes, please, tell us a story,' we answered in one voice.

'Do you know there is only one toilet for both men and women in the village?' Uncle Sun asked us.

'Yes, I know,' I tried to show off my knowledge.

'Do you know how to use it?' he asked, looking at me.

'I know, I know.' I shouted. 'You put your red belt on the wall, so others know you are in it,' I said.

'Yes, that's right,' Uncle Sun said, nodding, 'Once upon a time,' he continued, 'there was a schoolboy named Ugly Song. One morning, he saw his teacher go to the toilet a few times. He knew the teacher had diarrhoea.' Uncle Sun smiled at us and looked round to see if any adults were watching him telling a rude story. 'He put his red belt on the toilet wall and walked off.

When his teacher walked to the toilet, holding his pants, he saw the red belt. He went back to his room and waited. Then he went to the toilet again. "Oh, no, not another red belt." He moaned. He was agitated the whole morning. Ugly Song was laughing inside with his mates...' Uncle Sun made an agitated walking movement. Tiger and I laughed loudly and fell onto each other.

'What are you doing with the children?' Father turned around and yelled.

Tiger and I jumped and stopped laughing immediately.

'How can you be a chief for the Revolutionary Committee when you are still teasing little children? Be serious for a change!' Father's face was red with anger.

I knew the rule was that adults had to be respectable in front of children. But Father had told many dirty jokes himself and did not like Uncle Sun to do the same.

They finished the power-seizing plan. Now they just had to wait for the *Highest Order* from our great leader Chairman Mao.

On the evening of 22 January 1967, Father and Mother came home from work as usual.

They began cooking immediately without arguing who should start cooking first as they often did. I sensed they were going to have a revolutionary meeting that night. I was frightened to stay home with Tiger without my parents. But I couldn't complain because it was common for our parents to leave us home by ourselves. Sometimes my parents locked the door from outside.

Father was rolling the dough to make noodles. Mother was chopping up half of a bok choi. I was peeling potatoes. Mother asked, 'What do you think the 8 o'clock news will be tonight?'

Father said, 'I have a feeling that tonight is the night. I think we are going to seize power.'

'Just as well,' Mother said. 'The Radicals in Shanghai and Beijing have already had their go.'

Then we heard Uncle Wang's loud-as-a-thunder-clap voice, 'Revolutionary comrades,' he boomed, 'there is a revolutionary meeting tonight. Everyone has to attend!'

Uncle Wang had the grand title of Revolutionary Messenger for the Post Office Telecommunications compound – which meant that he had to call out messages for the revolutionary meetings.

Uncle Wang seemed like an ancient man. I knew two types of old people – those who were old, and those who were near death. If they still smiled from time to time, they were old. If they did not smile any more, they were near death. Uncle Wang certainly was the latter. Years later, I would find out that he wasn't as old as I thought – he just looked that way.

He had droopy, puffy eyes like a basset hound. He was nearly as tall as my grandpa, who was 188 centimetres tall. His back was slightly stooped, but he walked with giant steps.

Uncle Wang's actual job was to deliver the personal messages for the compound, because we did not have telephones in our houses. The entire compound only had one telephone – a black thing that lived in his room.

Three generations of compound residents had addressed him as Uncle Wang, even though he was related to none of us. He was very well respected for doing an excellent job of delivering the messages with his gigantic voice.

'Not a revolutionary meeting again?' I said. 'I'm afraid to stay home by myself.'

'What are you afraid of?' Mother asked.

'Ghosts.'

'Don't be silly, you know there are no ghosts in this world,' Mother scolded.

'Grandma said there is.'

'Has your grandma ever seen a ghost?'

'No.'

'Well?'

'Can you not lock the door from outside, so I can run out of the house if ghosts come?' I asked before they left.

Mother paused a moment and said, 'Ok, put this key around your neck and don't lose it.' Then they left.

It was getting dark. Tiger fell asleep, without a care in the world. I was scared and lonely. I could feel the hairs on the back of my neck rising.

Suddenly, the tiny space of our house overwhelmed me. If

the ghosts came inside, there was nowhere to run, nowhere to hide. Retrieving my day clothes from a nearby chair, I put on layer after layer of warm padded jackets and pants. I had to get outside where there was more space to run away.

I almost regretted my decision when the freezing Siberian wind swirled around me as I opened the door, but I had to get out because I could feel a woman ghost in pure white clothes was behind me. Everyone told stories about her.

As I walked around the compound, the chilly wind crept into my padded jacket, shivering in the cold. The ground was slippery with snow and ice. The sky was forlorn. The sun had shied away, as if, with misgivings. The moon and stars hid behind a wall of foreboding cloud. All the children had gone to bed, everything was quiet. A strong current of stiff air whipped loose hair about my face, blowing fine grit into my eyes.

I went back home, turning around every few steps to check for ghosts.

Back in the warmth of our house, I shut the door quickly so that the woman ghost could not slip in with me. Our door was not customarily locked. We never had thieves and intruders in our compound. During these times, even the intruders and thieves were busy with their own revolution, I guessed. I took off the piles of jackets and pants and snuggled next to Tiger and took refuge on our large bed and thought about death. What did dying feel like? What would the world be like if I died? My head began to ache from all the thinking. Then my eyelids became heavy, I fell asleep.

Father and Mother were at home the next morning when we woke up. Mother was cheerful.

'Why didn't you come home last night?' I asked.

'We went to seize power. We have the power now,' Mother said, with a gleam in her eye. 'The Radicals won!'

As Mother spoke, Father twisted and danced and walked in a silly way.

'I was right!' said Father, happy with himself. 'My prediction came true.'

Uncle Sun and other committee members came to our house in the middle of the day. Everyone was ecstatic, their eyes glowing and faces beaming.

'Last night was a glorious night, wasn't it?' Uncle Sun proclaimed in his loud voice.

Everyone nodded their heads in unison.

'We finally have the power of the Company!' Uncle Sun declared with his fists up.

Father said, 'Let's finish organising the Revolutionary Committee and make the announcement.'

But Uncle Sun was too happy. He turned round and said to Tiger, and me, 'Your mother. Don't think she is thin and small. She was the power snatching hero last night!'

I looked at Mother with such pride, my mother, the hero in power seizing. But I had no idea what Mother did. So, I waited until Uncle Sun and the rest of the committee members left our house and prepared to go to work in the offices that were previously occupied by Yang and other deputy directors to ask.

'What is power?' I asked. In Chinese the character power is quite abstract.

'Power is a stamp.'

'A stamp?' I asked looking at Mother, perplexed.

'Did you snatch a stamp?'

'Stamp here means official seals,' Father explained.

'I seized a lot of official seals,' declared Mother.

'Why? What would you do with them?' I asked.

'They are the power,' said Mother, with a serious look. 'You can give formal approvals to decisions.'

'How did you do it?' I asked Mother, excited.

'It was so crowded. Thousands of people from many companies came out to the Iron-Steel Road. We were in front of the city government building, drowned in the music of the Internationale. I tried to seize the power from Aunty Xing's hands, but she fought with me. I snatched it hard from her,' Mother said, matter-of-factly.

'Which official seals did you grab?' I asked.

'There were quite a lot of official seals, small ones, and big ones. The Conservatives collected all of them from the offices and put them into a small Post Office mailbag. They were going to run away with it.' Mother said, smiling.

I couldn't imagine adults physically snatching official seals, and it sounded a bit silly, wasn't that what little children do? I'd better not ask. I was only a small child who had lived all my life in the village. City folks were not the same.

'Did you all fight like Red Guards?' I asked.

'Yes, there were fights and scuffles. Some silly people threw rocks at each other and others hit people with sticks.'

'Where is this little bag of power now?'

'One of the members of the Revolutionary Committee hid it.'

'Where did he hide it?' I asked Mother.

'I can't tell you. You are only a child,' Mother said. Her face was delighted, and then closed.

Then another message blared from the loudspeaker that Radical groups in the entire country had seized power from the establishment within that period. Many Big-character posters were written and displayed. Struggle Meetings against the power holders were held everywhere. Real work was carried out at a minimal level – some other companies stopped work altogether. But Chairman Mao was thrilled that *rivers and mountains in our country were all red*. We had this slogan in red ink everywhere on our city walls.

I never had a chance to ask if they used that little bag of official seals because Uncle Sun, now a big shot, became cocky and refused to talk to me.

Since adults were having so much fun fighting over official seals, we children in the compound thought we should at least try it. The dilemma was we did not have any official seals to fight for. This did not hinder us from doing our bit for the glorious power-snatching revolution, and not even the cold wind and frozen ground could prevent us. We put on our homemade wadded jackets, trousers, shoes and mittens. We marched to the centre of our compound.

Then we just stood in two groups opposite each other. All of a sudden, Lingqing shouted, 'Big Blockhead!' our nickname for one girl in the Conservative Faction. Our group followed, 'Big Blockhead!'

'Sour-dough Face!' shouted a big girl from the opposite crowd about a girl in our crowd who had loose skin on her face.

'Sour-dough Face!' their group repeated.

'Big *Bi* Meng!' called New China, using a crude word for *vagina*, for my friend who had a large mouth.

Zhiling Gao

Golden

The years fold into each other
Like worn pages of a book,
Fingers once strong and steady
Now tremble with time.
The faces that once looked down
Now turn upward
As we stand taller.
We grew up
Under their watchful eyes,
Their hands guiding us
Through uncertain days.
Now, we watch them
Slow their pace,
Their steps more careful,
Their voices are softer.
Time moves quietly
Until it doesn't,
And we realise
We are the bridge
Between what was
And what will be,
Holding onto their hands
As they once held ours,
Grateful for each moment
That still lingers.

Amanda Divers

Globalisation!

Globalisation, schmobalisation: So who cares what they call it all I know is that starting next week I have no more job.

"What are you saying Heimy, they gave you the sack?" Rebecca asked her husband?

"Yes the boss called me and some of my colleagues to his office this morning, and after a long speech, none of us made heads or tails off , we were told that he was obliged to dispense with our services. He said that he was most upset to have to come to this decision, but in order to become more competitive with the rest of the world, tough measures had to be taken."

"But Henry you have been with the firm 10 years since its inception. How can they do this to you?"

"Well from what I understand, a machine is going to do my work from now on, a machine Rebecca . I spent 10 years of my life working for this firm, not knowing I was a machine."

"My poor Heimy and how are we going to survive If you lose your job. How will we be able to pay the instalments on our house, on our car and with Tania's wedding in two months time? How will our daughter feel if we can no longer afford to give her a proper wedding and reception as we planned?"

"Don't worry Rebecca, nothing will change regarding our beloved Tania's wedding, even if I have to work as a kitchen hand or a garbage collector in the meantime. The boss promised us a small amount of cash in compensation, but he did not mention how much."

"God willing, I may find another job that is, if other firms have not followed the trend of replacing people by damned computers."

"Don't forget Heimy you are now 48 years old. Do you think they will hire you at your age? From what I hear they are only employing young people now."

"Experience, experience Rebecca. What about experience? Does it count for nothing?"

"Will they hire a young schlemiel just fresh from uni to do a man's job? I am still fit and able with all my faculties intact. Leave this to me Rebecca . Starting tomorrow, I'm going to apply for a position in as many companies as I can."

Rebecca shook her head and said nothing. What could she say? Heimy was clever and presented well. Maybe someone would appreciate a man with experience rather than a younger person with none.

Heimy sent hundreds of letters, put his name down in several employment agencies, even knocked on company doors. He was given the same answer everywhere. Firms were retrenching people instead of hiring new staff. GLOBALISATION!

This cursed word again! Save money, be competitive, computers! How can machines deal with customers the way human beings do? Heimy was at a loss to understand. Technology was necessary, but could never replace face-to-face contact with people, answer their queries their questions. Can you imagine a person's frustration when dealing with this impersonal voice over the phone if you want… Press one, if you… press 2 and so on.

I wonder how uncle Harry, a seventy year-old and other retirees like him, could deal with such a crazy system? What was the world coming to? Will humans have to become robots to find a job?

Despair was what he felt now! The money he got from his firm after ten years of faithful service was just enough to cover some of the pressing expenses and Tania's wedding.

His pride was too great to go on unemployment benefits.

Me ! Go begging from the government? Never!

Rebecca decided to go to work. In the papers, they were asking for cleaners. This did not require speaking fluent English. Heimy was devastated. He has always been the sole breadwinner. He had never allowed Rebecca to work before. They were never rich, but they always manage to bring up the children, Tania and Maury well and there was always food on the table. Yes, he always work hard since they arrived in Australia from Russia, almost 13 years ago. Fortunately, he had studied English in Moscow, and had no trouble finding a job on arrival. His brother Zach was the lucky one. They had left Russia at the same time, but Zach had chosen to go to the United States instead, and he was doing very well working for a large company there.

As time passed Heimy sank deeper and deeper into depression. He managed to find casual jobs here in there to make ends meet but he felt useless, despondent he had lost his self-respect. His son Maury who was doing his VCE.this year did not recognise his dear father. Where was the jovial papa he used to know? He missed the happy family outings in the country every weekend, the friends who came to visit. Now his father never wanted to go out or receive anyone at home. He systematically refused invitations, even from his closest and dearest friends. His married daughter, Tania and her new husband, Sam, where the only visitors he would tolerate.

"Heimy darling, is it your fault if you cannot find a job?" asked Rebecca? "Why do you blame yourself for something that is out of your control? Please, listen to me. I'm happy to work and you are doing your best. We are managing ok, so for our sake try to accept the situation. One day I'm sure something will turn up. There are others who are worse off than we," are implored Rebecca.

Heimy didn't answer. He just left the room, dragging his feet like an old man.

One day the family received a letter from Heimy's brother from America. He was announcing his visit to Australia for the following month. In his letter, he asked how are the prospects of work here as he and his family were thinking of maybe trying to settle in Australia as he had just lost his executive position with his company in the US. He said that everywhere they were retrenching people due to this crazy new concept called globalisation!

Heimy and the family who were sitting around the table for Sabbath dinner that evening, all burst in uncontrollable laughter. They just could not stop repeating GLOBALISATION GLOBALISATION!

"Do you realise Rebecca," said Heimy still laughing, "Zach, the family brains, the one who swore to make a fortune in the United States, my clever brother, who held a high corporate position in his company, retrenched just like me on account of this damned GLOBALISATION!

Heimy never complained or felt depressed ever again!

Jenny Chevalier

Swimming deeper for the real jewels

In a dream, in a tunnel, in the middle of the night
Through murky and troubled waters I have been
In my mind I have swum through the depths
I swam a bit deeper, found the treasures of wisdom, secrets and wishes
I swam deeper to rid myself of certain people
Situations and people that are on the shore with their delusions and negative ways that I know for sure
The wiser more knowledgeable ones also think that
I suppose some are unaware of living in kinder, wiser ways
Some have been hurt themselves
Some not know any better
These are some of the gifts I give myself apart from the knowledge of the wiser ones
For the significance of them is important to me
All while swimming deeper in the ocean of my mind
To rid me of this illusionary world for just a while, to get through this life in a better state of being
How nice it is to be in a better state of being even for just a while
Swimming for the real jewels of wisdom, happiness is one of the jewels
Things more profound, giving more meaning to this life

Rose Lumbaca Crane

Surgery

It's like this:
if I have the guts to lend myself
to a scalpel for an afternoon,
then I have them enough
to be mean when it's needed.
But fickleness is a second helping from the bench, the
residue of my achievements trickling down my chin,
I'm a contortionist only sometimes.
I'll be breaking my knees
on a backwards mouse wheel
and waving my palm sideways in dismissal, like
I can walk and excavate without an identity under me.
I'm no archaeologist,
but I'll watch the nice people
walking to their nice houses and breathe softly
out my nose like I grieve for them in secret
between the plywood walls of an office cubical.
I do grieve for them anyway, of course.
Caught between the end of a meal,
the end of beginning,
and the back of a knife.
Like a hamster,
like a patient.

Lucy Tomov

Waiting

Inside the isolated country cottage, Elly tosses and turns. It's late, and surprisingly hot seeing summer's almost over. She can't sleep because her baby, due in four days, will not stop kicking. Her husband Tom has nicknamed it Boxer.

Outside, the road is deserted. A car hasn't passed for hours. Tom is in town working on another editorial deadline. He's been caught up in a heated, political controversy about planning permits she finds boring. It's the last time he'll work late at the newspaper before the baby arrives, but he's said this before. She's known him all her life. They grew up next door ato each other, and she understands his dedication to work. Still, his career is on track, and in six months, they'll go back to Melbourne.

Elly has been trying to sleep for hours, but finding a comfortable position is difficult. She's had what her mother calls a dream pregnancy, and because they've had such fun buying things for the nursery, she now wonders why they waited so long to have a baby. Her case has been packed for weeks. She can see it standing to attention in the corner of the bedroom, like a good soldier, and like her, waiting.

An hour passes, and the bedroom feels like a furnace. Boxer is still dancing to his or her own inner rhythm, and it's difficult to breathe. She rolls out of bed and goes to the window. Tom has never liked her leaving it open when she's alone. He can be so silly sometimes. She looks out and sees little. Even the moon seems to have deserted her tonight. Then she hears the hoot of the owl who lives in the trees opposite, and feels comforted another living thing is awake in this lonely place.

The wire door creaks as Elly pushes it open. Fresh air is what she needs, but as she steps onto the veranda, she breathes in the foul smell coming from the tannery up the road instead. It's really bad tonight, she thinks. That's probably why the rent is so cheap, and has nothing to do with the rumours in town. Some people, she's found, can be so superstitious.

She shuffles along the veranda in her bare feet, avoiding from memory the broken planks, and as she eases herself into the sagging hammock, she hears the owl's screech a second time. And then a third, louder. Why so talkative tonight old girl, she thinks.

Elly looks towards the trees, and for a moment senses a movement beyond the open gate. Probably a cat, or a rabbit. She feels too drowsy to care because Boxer has stopped kicking at last. She smiles, rubs her stomach lovingly, and closes her eyes against the dark. Peace at last. It is then that she smells the smoke, and feels rough unfamiliar hands around her neck.

Sandra Lanteri

A wartime letter of love and loss

During the post war years young Szaja had a florid affair with a novice nun, Christine. They were separated when he left Switzerland for Paris. She was to follow once she escaped the clutches of the monastery and her parents. After many weeks of separation Szaja received a telegram to tell him Christine had taken her life. Eighty years later a letter arrives at the museum where Szaja volunteers.

S.C.
c/o the Melbourne Museum
Private

Ma très chère Szaja, cette lettre vous surprendra, j'espère pas un choc, car vous verrez que je suis toujours en vie. Je n'ai pas péri de mes propres mains il y a toutes ces années . . .

My dearest Szaja, this letter will come as a surprise to you, I hope not a shock, for you will see that I am still alive. I did not perish by my own hand all those years ago.

You must wonder why I have chosen to write to you, now that we have entered the twilight years of our time on this earth. Should I have left you to think what you had been told by letter as you waited for me to join you in Paris? Perhaps? For better or worse I have decided to write to you. We have each spent a lifetime and lived through our loves and losses.

I start by saying that I never abandoned my love for you, not ever. I cherished our time together from the very moment when we first met, when I prepared reports for the Red Cross. My love grew like the flowers of a spring garden, each petal of a different colour, of a different dimension beaconing the warmth of the sun, and on show for all to see. And that is what happened. The nuns became suspicious that something had changed within me. My mood, my energy, the clarity of my eyes sent a signal. Coupled with our weekly letters to each other suspicions were raised by the nun who handled our mail. But I was young and naïve and suspected nothing of the convent when your letters stopped arriving. I kept writing to you, at first making excuses for your lack of response, however, as time wore on, I became more and more despondent, stopped eating and fell into a deep melancholy. Months passed; yet I never doubted our love for one another.

As it happened, one of the senior sisters was to travel to Paris for business and she asked if I would accompany her. She said it would be good for me and helpful to her. At first, cautious due to my depressed state, I hesitated but Sister was quite insistent, and I accepted her offer.

During journey from Zurich to Paris, Sister and I spoke, first about the mundane and then, I gave in to her warmth and trust. I had held back, kept our affair to myself for so long. It was as if a dam wall burst, and amongst my tears and sobs, I unburdened my heart. I talked about our innocence at Red Cross interviews, how we eventually fell into each other's arms, how we made love and promised to be with each other in Paris. When I told her your mail abruptly stopped, like a sentence being cut off mid-way, she raised an eyebrow and told me there may not be an innocent reason for this, perhaps the convent post office was not to be trusted.

Sister was firm with her advice. She said I could not share my heart between Jesus and you, dear Szaja; I needed to resolve the situation. And that, when we reach Paris, we will track you down and that I should see where my heart leads.

The prospect of seeing you again spun my emotions in a whirlwind, cycling from elation and excitement to love, to a fear of finding and loosing you again. Sister saw my turmoil and calmed me. She said we will attend to this before we see to the convent business.

From your letters I knew you spent time in cafes on Rue de Rosier, sometimes visiting the hidden park, as you called it. This is where we began our search. Two nuns dressed in black in the heart of the Marais, the Jewish Quarter.

We went from café to café, trying our best not to be observed by the patrons.

And there you were. Sitting at a small table on the sidewalk in front of a café.

Sister held me back from rushing forward. Wait, she said, he is there with a girl. Just the two of them.

It took all my strength to resist falling into your arms, to stand back, to observe, to try to make out what was happening. Sister maintained her firm grip on my arm that she interlocked with hers and suggested we remain at a distance.

The pair of you seemed very comfortable with each other. She leaning forward, hand on chin, eyes fixed on you, absorbing every word uttered and every nuanced expressed. You, animated, capturing her gaze, never looking away. She, placing her open palm on the table. You, reaching for her hand. Fingers intertwined.

Together you rose from the table and headed towards the entrance to the hidden garden. We followed. I watched you both lying on a grassy patch, wrapped in each other's arms, warmed by sun.

I was lost in a sea of emotions. I despaired that you had found another love. My feelings of love for you were spiralling to dejection and anger.

Sister dragged me away, telling me that we should return to our room where we can distil what we had seen and make a plan.

I took to my bed to pray the Holy Rosary, to meditate, to look for answers. By evening I was calm, it was time to speak with Sister. I told her prayer had revealed the path foreword. You had found a new love, a new place for your heart. I could not create further misery for my own gratification. I would withdraw back to the convent, in the knowledge that you were happy. I would never lose my love for you.

Some time later, on our return to the convent, Sister did some investigation at the post office. She disclosed to me her findings. The post office comptroller Sister had been asked to withhold the mail between us, and to end your persistent letters, she was to send an official note telling you I had taken my life.

You were easy to find, and I chose to send this long letter as private correspondence to you at the museum. After all a museum is a place for memories. I don't wish to disrupt your life. It is up to you whether you share the information with your family or not.

I am poorly now and do not believe I have much more time.

Forever, love, Christine.

Warren Fineberg

Bliss of declutter

There she was, dear Elizabeth, standing in the middle of her living room and totally overwhelmed by all her possessions. I was there with her.

Some were beautiful, valuable ornaments and others were simply just clutter.

The moment had arrived for her to do something about it. She is totally ready for it and I am there to help her.

She chose me to help her because she knew I understood the sentiments and emotions which are kindled by letting go of precious possessions. She also knew that I was an Interior Designer by profession and therefore I could advise her how to improve a room aesthetically. And she regarded me as a good trusted friend.

Over the years she had accumulated many books and magazines and because she was a teacher, she had kept them all as reference material.

Also, her love of souvenirs from her travels made her home extra exotic with all the amazing artwork, ornaments, small objects and interesting furniture.

But for an outsider it looked more like an extravagant little boutique museum.

Elizabeth used to love entertaining and organising exquisite dinner parties with the gourmet dishes she had learnt from all the different countries she had travelled to. Everybody felt so special to receive an invitation.

And I was one of her favourite guests.

She was such a charming host – everybody loved her. Her intellect, her charisma, her beautiful feminine dress style - I could never get enough of this gorgeous, witty British lady. She was simply the best communicator and listener I have experienced in all my life. Our interests were so aligned with each other.

But now we need to get back to work.

"Getting started is always the hardest part" I said.

The plan was to tackle one room at a time. Elizabeth agreed cheerfully. The big lounge was our starting point.

The process was slow but also fun. Each item had a treasure trove of memories. I loved to listen to her wonderful storytelling. The act of letting go of objects wasn't just about that, it was also about releasing the past and making room for new possibilities.

By the end of the weekend her home was transformed into an open, spacious, even more beautiful house where you could wander freely and enjoy the new light and beauty of her abode. She felt blissfully happy with this outcome and so did I. Elizabeth gave me some lovely ornaments which I will cherish to the end of my days.

Monika Nuesch

The absolute limit

I'll bump the rail when I'm angry and
ricochet off to the other side of the track.
Bone marrow weighted and
spine leaden. Calcification a
natural consequence of staying
in the same place, for much too long.
See, I'm not very good at being wronged.
Justification is a sore bandage and I
have never been a graceful healer,
but I do know this.
After you, I will not spend days wistful
against the atrocity of feeling.
I will not detail the track marks of my soul against
the back door in prayer for a saviour.
Horrified at the state of my organs,
begging for a sensible delay.
You didn't mean to teach me I was
without consequence. But you did.
I didn't mean to believe you. But I did.
We didn't mean for it to happen. But it did.
Now I look back and wonder what you told me,
to make me think
I deserved any of it.

Lucy Tomov

War vigil

hearts heave
souls in sorrow
murmurs
mourning
grief

        empty places at the table

sadness
silence
lost

        blind with pain

hope
shielded from death
a tiny girl child
saved
brave mother
dead

        forever

Ann Simic

The power of helping

Just read a meme from the pen of Akira Kurasawa, the outstanding film producer. Heard it about ten years ago.

I had a wonderful friend who used to invite me to dinner, because I was on my own.

One day, she asked if I would take out her overseas visitor, so she could cook without her being at home. I decided to taker her to The Gallery at Federation Square.

We enjoyed it right up until closing time.

Suddenly she asked if ACMI was still open. It was! We hurried across the Square to perceive an exhibition like nother.

How lucky am I to be always rewarded for helping.

Dita Gould

So this is love, I think silently, out loud

So this is love, I think silently, out loud.
We are two, completely alone, as one.
The both of us, bound separately together.
Feeding off, feasting, starving one another.
I thought myself incapable of this shallow depth.
In you I have found perfect imperfection- my reversed reflection.
The one who has the capacity to misunderstand
me so completely that they mistreat, misinterpret,
misrepresent me almost as malevolently as I do myself.
So this is love, I say out loud, silently.

Jennifer Baker

Haiku for a frangipani

Yellow throated queen
frangipani - Bali's joy
your scent sings to me

Grey trunk gnarled and old
Petals sit so young and fresh
Youth and age as one

Blossom letting go
Falling to the arms of earth
Your brief glory spent

Sharon Hurst

Spring River crossing

"If we don't get moving first thing today, the Spring River will be in flood," said John. "It could take three to four days to go down, and then we'd miss the Western Arthurs."

These were the culmination of our two-week trip through South-west Tasmania; a week around the South Coast to port Davey; across the Bathurst Narrows by rowing boat; a long slog to the base of the Western Arthurs, and then up into the crags, the high moors, and the multi-coloured lakes along the most spectacular range in the south-west. I had waited years to do this trip.

The Arthurs run diagonally across the path of the Roaring Forties, which strike south-west Tasmania with their full force, giving it the highest rainfall in Australia. Torrential rain had trapped us for two days at Bathurst Narrows, but now it was only drizzling as we started walking.

The first creek we came to was already swollen; we crossed waist-deep, using poles to brace ourselves against the current. The next was running at chest-height, and we crossed together diagonally, holding a branch upstream against us to steady ourselves.

An hour later, long before we expected it, the track disappeared under water.

"I was afraid of this," said John. "The river's broken its banks. These are the outer flood-waters – the actual crossing's a mile on to the north."

We splashed on, John uncharacteristically quiet, then Hank, a gentle even-tempered Mormon, nearly seven feet tall, and untroubled by anything: a man simply happy to be walking in the bush. I was next, and last came Peter, wiry but strong, the youngest in our party.

Now we were wading through timber, the sky blotted out, and the water beginning to swirl around the trunks. The trees were hung with mosses, and fallen branches tangled everywhere. Soon, we couldn't walk on the ground any longer; we made our way along fallen trees and branches, debris of earlier floods, stepping cautiously from each log to the next, sometimes above, sometimes just below the swirling waters. It grew deeper and darker. Poles thrust down now longer touched the bottom, and the current, even here, far from the river, was flowing strongly.

Getting from tree to tree became more difficult. Hank went over a long sunken log and called from the other side: "Anne, grab hold of this branch when you can reach it – I'll help you over." I stepped slowly across, reaching out for it. But the branch was old and rotten; it snapped between us, and I was under the black water, choking and fighting, eyes, ears and throat filled with muddy darkness, as my pack slipped higher on to my neck, driving me down, drowning me in full consciousness.

Suddenly I was free. A giant hand had plucked me out, pack and all, and set me down in safety. Shivering, I watched the others cross, Hank helping them over with an arm like a gorilla. This man was indestructible: he would save us all.

To go back was now impossible; the rising waters had drowned the logs behind us. The main river, crashing and thundering, was just ahead. But where was the crossing – the log bridge and the chain?

"Last year they were fifteen feet above the river," said John desperately. Now they had gone. We knew how swiftly the rivers rose, but I'd never imagined anything like this.

"We can't stay here – it's still rising". With no idea where the track was, we swung and pulled ourselves upstream. The far bank was high; between it and our flooded tree-world, a white torrent thundered, sweeping everything before it.

"Look – we can cross, up there!"

A huge tree had crashed across the river, high at each end, water foaming over it in the centre.

"Wait!" shouted John.

But it was too late. Hank was already out on the trunk, stepping slowly down, arms outstretched for balance. Just where the river swept the log, he turned inexplicably to speak to us. To our horror, he began to rock, backwards and forwards, facing downstream, a look of terror on his big mild face. Slowly, he fell, backwards into the torrent, his rucksack dragging him down. Somehow, he surfaced, arms flailing, the current forcing him against the log. He flung his arms over it and hung there, roaring like a bull: "HELP ME! HELP ME!" Years later, I can still see him, his eyes staring, his mouth open, roaring above the thunder of the river.

Peter had his pack off already, and was astride the log, pulling himself out on his buttocks; John followed. Hank was blind with fear. They wrestled with Hank's rucksack, shoulder-deep in the foaming water and dragged it onto the log: then they heaved on his belt, trying to haul him up. Hank struggled and kicked, grunting with the enormous effort of unplugging himself from the drag of the current. Minutes later, trembling and exhausted, we were all back in the trees – the log still our only path to safety.

"We'll have to cross it sitting down", said John. "Undo your hip-buckles, and if you go in, fall upstream, for Chrissake!"

So one by one, we crossed on our bottoms, thighs deep in icy water on either side. Hands forward – pull. Hands forward – slowly – pull. Our legs were ripped by the spikes along log, but we were over. On dry ground.

For two hours on the other side, we hacked our way with compass and machete through the melaleuca scrub, the tough white trunks only inches apart.

Twilight was drifting down when at last we emerged onto button-grass. The track, not twenty yards to our left, snaked away over the spongy plains.

Oh, the warmth of our sleeping bags. Tomorrow, the Western Arthurs. Tonight, sleep …..

Anne Sedgley

Day's end

Twilight glows through
sun-drenched clouds.
Dark dragons cast shadows.
Tree-studded headland,
pencil-slender sentries
in green, gleam, glint,
blaze, bask in day's end;
link earth and shy sky,
reflect in receding waves.

Long yawning stretch of smooth sand.
Lone person.

Ann Simic

The intriguing life story of Madame Dulac

A magical story inspired by the patriarchal society which has always existed since time began and partly exists in some parts of the world even today.

"What a lovely day!" exclaimed Violette.

The Parisian sky never appeared so blue, the sun so warming on this lovely autumn day in 1889. Yvette shunned the coachman who stopped to ask if she wanted a ride to her destination.

"Oh, no Monsieur, today I have decided to walk and enjoy this autumn breeze.

She wore her very best blue Sunday dress, very tight at the waist, with her velvet cape, and same colour bonnet. Her fur mittens kept her hands cosy and warm

"You are quite right, madame. "Bonne journée" (have a good day) he replied with a smile.

There were not too many people out this morning, only a few carriages. One could hear the sound of horses' hooves on the cobblestones.

Violette hastened her step; she was on the way to the new museum she had read about the night before. So, without hesitation she had decided that today was the day to do so. On the way a sudden urge came over her that she had to reach the museum faster. The museum offered a collection of ancient works of art, paintings, sculptures, wax figures, scenes of life in past centuries, and a lot more. She normally never ventured out from her neighbourhood, she always shopped in boutiques in her area where she was always greeted cheerfully by the owners.

"Bonjour Madame Dulac, deux baguettes bien croustillantes pour vous comme d'habitude?"

Monsieur Latour, the baker always reserved the crunchiest baguettes for her.

Monsieur Laurent, the butcher, also kept aside for her every Thursday the best cut of veal for the blanquette, a very delicious veal stew.

On Saturdays, market day, she wandered along the stalls, picking some delicacy here and there for the Sunday lunch.

So, on the evening before, on reading the advertisement in the paper, she felt an uncontrollable urge to visit this new museum which was situated in the Marais district, not too far from home. Today, she somehow felt very bold for the first time in her life.

Violette Dulac was married and had four children. She was still attractive but her life with Emile was very trying and boring. Her whole days were taken up with looking after the household and the children. Emile, her husband had very quickly lost interest in her as a woman. They still occasionally made love, but the whole thing was over in a minute, and afterwards he would turn his back at her and start snoring. A very thrilling experience! He considered her more like à chattel, a servant whose only role in life was to look after him, and eventually the children when they came.

He was always critical of her however hard she tried to please him.

He often abused her without any valid reason if the meal

was a few minutes late when he got home.

"I work hard for you and the children; you are home all day, a lady of leisure, and you cannot even find the time to have the meal ready and the children out of sight when I come home tired from work?"

A lady of leisure indeed! Who got up first thing in the morning, prepared breakfast for everyone, took the older children to school, the younger twins to *la maternelle*, the pre-school, did the shopping , the cleaning, the washing, the dusting, the cooking and so much more. She hated arguments, so she never complained. She resigned herself to her life although she thought that if her husband would spend more time at home with her and the children who really needed to see and know their father better, life would be more bearable.

He came home for dinner after work and left straight after to join his friends at the cafe Flore where he always spent his evenings playing belote, a card game before coming home drunk and in a bad mood if he lost at the game.

Sunday was the only day they went to church as a family.

Violette was a good person, but weak of character so Emile took advantage of that trait in her to bully her and constantly put her down.

What could she do anyway? With no means of her own? Where could she go, an orphan, having lost her parents during the war? She was totally dependent on Emile as after all, in those days France as many other countries was à patriarchal society. With time she lost hope of a better life and even started neglecting her appearance.

She felt dull and unattractive.

Today she felt unusually cheerful though as she finally arrived at her destination. She bought her ticket and entered the museum. A feeling of excitement overwhelmed her. This, for her was no ordinary day. Emile's bad temper, the chores awaiting her. Nothing seems to matter anymore. It was *her* day!

She started the visit by admiring the gallery of portraits. Famous people from past centuries who seemed to stare at her. Grand ladies beautifully attired. Gentlemen in their glorious uniforms. Violette was impressed. She visited different rooms, some depicting how was life in the past centuries: a wax family in their living room, the mother embroidering on the settee, the father at his desk working, the children sitting on the floor with their governess reading or playing. It appeared that life was more family orientated in those days, Violette thought with a feeling of envy.

Other rooms displayed elegant furniture, sculptures and paintings so fashionable among the aristocracy, the rich and famous. Everything delighted her.

She continued her walk along the corridor until she reached the last room, a beautifully furnished lady's boudoir. A statue of a woman dressed in a white lace corsage and bouffant satin skirt with ribbons, flowers and various ornaments which were fashionable two centuries ago in the high Parisian society, was standing in an alcove in the corner.

Violette looked at her face and gasped! God, she looks so much like ... me...! Yet she looks more stunningly beautiful and radiant, she thought. It was uncanny. There was a difference though. The expression differed from Violette's gentle face, this woman's expression was very determined and also a little hard. Who was she? She wondered? Violette could not help wanting to touch her. She screamed as she touched this woman's face. It's impossible, she thought, the skin felt warm and alive! This cannot be true; this woman is a dummy made of wax. I am imagining things. She forced herself to touch her face again and this time she cried out with horror as she felt again that the skin was warm and very much alive!

Suddenly, as if someone compelled her to do so, she touched the woman's head. Suddenly, like magic, the wig fell from the woman onto Violette's head.

At that moment everything started spinning around Violette. She fainted and fell on the floor.

"Looks like she is coming to," a voice was saying.

Violette opened her eyes and looked around her, she was lying on a sofa. She sat up and stared at the figure in the alcove and with a triumphant smile, she got up and without even a glance at all the commotion around her, she casually left the room, walked back to the entrance and disappeared into the street.

She reached her house and entered. Her children were standing there waiting for her. It was so unusual for their mother not to be there to greet them when they came back from school and *La Maternelle*. The older children always picked the little ones up on their way home.

One of the older children stared at her and said, "Mamani, you look so different today!"

Violette smiled and went to her room, locked the door and stood in front of the mirror.

Her blond hair fell loosely around her face, her green eyes sparkled like emeralds. Her skin was as smooth as silk.

"I am beautiful!" she said, "gone is the weak and vulnerable woman. I will show what a woman like me can achieve in this day and age."

She heard her husband come in the front door.

"What is this mess? Where is your mother?" he asked the children. "Violette come here at once, you hear?"

Violette came out of her room and stood motionless at the door.

Emile looked at her and gasped.

"Violette, is that you? You seem changed!"

He could not believe his eyes. Was this unbelievably attractive woman his wife? Has he been blind to her beauty before?

He suddenly felt the urge to take her in his arms and walked towards her.

She smiled languidly and pulled him into the bedroom.

The next day Violette opened her door and called out to the children to come over as their dad had just suddenly passed away.

The funeral took place the next day.

There were many famous cabarets in Paris where people enjoyed music, laughter drink and dancing to the sound of an accordion. One in particular. called *La jarretière* "(the garter) was very famous and frequented by high society.

Violette decided to have fun and started to go to this cabaret every evening.

As soon as she entered, she was surrounded by most male patrons. They all succumbed to her charm and continually competed for her attention. She became the darling of this cabaret.

On occasion she would leave the establishment with one of the gentlemen in his carriage.

Some rumours started circulating in town and in the papers

that several men were found dead in the morning by their valet. It was as if they died in their sleep with no apparent cause, even after undergoing an autopsy. There were no signs of foul play: gun wounds, knife attacks or poison.

It seemed that they all died a natural death.

After a while the police were called to investigate. Too many men suffered the same fate.

Inspecteur Leblanc was put in charge of the investigation.

He somehow knew that these men were murdered. This was no coincidence, but how did they die?

The thought was keeping him awake nights on end He discovered, however, that all these gentlemen shared something in common. They had left the cabaret the evening before their death, accompanied by a well-known very attractive lady.

One evening Inspecteur Leblanc went incognito to *La jarretière*.

He looked around him and his attention was attracted by the laughter of a woman sitting at a table drinking and chatting with a number of admiring men. She was indeed very attractive with her flowing blond hair, green eyes and charm. Her laughter alone could drive any man out of his mind. Not me, he thought, I am too much in love with my Justine!

This woman must be the one I am looking for. There is something about her that is sending a shiver down my spine, a veiled cruel expression on her face.

He decided to stay and wait for her to leave. He waited till dawn until finally everyone started to leave. She also came out, but not on her own. She was accompanied by a gentleman. They both left together in his coach.

Inspecteur Leblanc hailed another coach and instructed the coachman to follow them.

Their coach stopped in front of a beautiful mansion.

But this is the residence of the Comte du Barry, I don't know what to do, he thought!

Shall I warn him of his impending fate?

However, I have no proof and will he believe me? He looks completely under the charm of this woman, who seems to have diabolical powers.

Of course not!

Let's hope that nothing will happen to him.

Against his will, the Inspecteur wrote down the address and left.

His intuition was correct. The next morning, the news came out that the Comte du Barry was discovered dead in his bed,

Inspecteur Leblanc blamed himself.

He felt so guilty not to have warned the Comte but could he have saved the Comte?

Through his investigation, he discovered Violette Dulac's address and decided to pay her a visit.

"I am sorry to disturb you Madame, I am Inspecteur Leblanc and would like to have a few words with you if it is convenient."

"May I come in?" he asked as she opened the door.

"Of course, Inspecteur, if you don't mind me being in my negligee."

"Not at all Madame, we, in the police force are used to everything. I only would like to ask you certain questions."

"I must tell you that I followed you last Monday when you accompanied Le Comte du Barry at his home. The next morning he was discovered dead. You must also be aware that during the last few months, several gentlemen were found dead in the morning after going home the night before accompanied by a mysterious lady, whom I suspect to be you Madame Dulac."

"Inspecteur, I do not deny that many gentlemen had invited me to their place for a nightcap. I did not stay very long as the coach was waiting to take me home.

I do not see any harm in that. I had nothing to do with their death. How dare you for coming into my house accusing me of murder? Do you have any proof, am I responsible for their death?"

"Unfortunately, not. I have no doute that you are guilty, but to be honest, I am baffled as to the way you went about it.

"I know it's very naive of me to ask you such a question," continued the inspecteur "but I beg you to put me out of my misery and tell me how you did commit these murders, because I know you did it, without leaving any trace?"

Madame Dulac sniggered and said "You make me laugh, Monsieur Inspecteur, however I am going to confess to you alone that yes, I am responsible for the death of these gentlemen but you will never be able to indict me as, I assure you, no one will ever discover how they died."

"Can you at least, tell me the reason why you committed these crimes?"

"Revenge my dear man! We, women have suffered so much by the hands of most men that, it's about time they pay the price for their misdeeds. Now please leave this house, I am extremely tired and I need to rest."

The inspecteur got up and walked to the door. As he reached it, he turned around and looking at her and said,

"Yes, I am leaving now but rest assured that we will see each other again. I promise you, Madame, this is not the end of it."

"Ha ha ha!" she replied bursting out laughing.

A few days later Madame Dulac received a summons to attend the *prefecture* (the police station) the following Tuesday morning.

On the day she entered inspecteur Leblanc's office. He was sitting at his desk writing. He beckoned her to sit down and continued to write for a minute or two.

"Inspecteur. You asked me to cone in this morning. Well, here I am. Now stop writing and tell me the reason I was summoned to come here today. Surely the situation has not changed has it?" she said ironically.

He slowly lifted his head and stared at her.

"On the contrary, Madame. I have a very good idea how you went about murdering these gentlemen. First may I offer you a glass of this special liqueur I always keep here to enjoy at times.? This is going to be a very long session."

"Yes, thank you. This is also my favourite drink. I do want you to know, however that I am no fool and am fully aware that you are not more advanced in your investigation than last time at my place," she said looking straight at him without flinching.

She started sipping her drink, enjoying the mellow taste in her mouth.

"Well, Monsieur Inspecteur, I'm listening. So tell me what did you discover?"

She suddenly felt her head spinning. "What…did…you ..put …in ..my ..drink?

"You have just drunk a very powerful poison and you will

die. I thought that is a just punishment for your misdeeds. Your day of judgement has arrived and now you will have to answer to your Maker," he said.

Madame Dulac, a horrified look on her face, started to lose consciousness, slipping from her chair onto the floor.

When Madame Dulac opened her eyes, she felt very strange. I must be dead she thought, where am I?

Two figures both dressed in floating white robes were hovering over her.

"Follow us! This is your day of judgement. The highest Court is awaiting you.

Trembling, she followed them in an eerie courtroom. The judge was sitting high up on a platform also dressed in flowing white robes with a hood over his head

"Bring the sinner closer please."

The two figures grabbed her by the arms and approached the platform.

"Now speak. State your name and your date and place of birth," he commanded in a stern voice.

She hesitated and looked around her and saw several figures sitting in their white robes as if also awaiting judgement

"Your name!" he shouted.

"My name is Marie . I was born in the small village of Tiers in 1679."

"You committed many crimes Marie and you will rot in hell for ever and ever. However, if during your lifetime, there were special circumstances that compelled you to act in this fashion, we may reconsider and alleviate your sentence.

"For your defence, accused, we have to hear in this Court

of Divine Justice your life story, speak now summoned the Judge. We may find some mitigating circumstances if you tell the truth."

Marie gulped and proceeded to recount every aspect of her existence.

"I was born in a dysfunctional family. We were very poor I had three brothers and a sister. My father was a drunken and violent man. He used to abuse and beat us all, including my poor mother, regularly. I swore that as soon as I grow up, I would leave my family and make a new life for myself. I knew I was beautiful as all the men around were attracted to me. It was then that I decided that I would make them pay a high price for their misdeeds, starting by my own father whom I murdered so that my family would live in peace.

"I started frequenting the best cabarets around and soon became the most sought-after and kept woman in town. Men showered me with expensive jewellery and money. Nothing however, stopped me from eliminating them my own way without ever being found out. That was my revenge for how they mistreated and hurt their family as well of all of us women. I hated them.

"I treated them with contempt and swore to make them pay for all the suffering my mother, myself and the rest of my family had to bear."

"You therefore admit that you committed murders in your lifetime.?

"And who is Violette Dulac?

My great grandchild. She was weak and miserable. Her husband treated her so badly that I had to avenge her by returning to earth and inhabiting her body. We looked alike so it was easy to impersonate her and get rid of the man, the cause of her suffering."

"So, you continued the life you led through Violette's and committed similar murders, didn't you?"

"Yes, as men these days had not changed even two centuries later. They deserved to die."

"Now Marie tell us how did you kill these men?"

"No, this is my secret. I will never be revealing it to anyone."

"Bring this woman's last victim over here!" commanded the judge.

A floating figure was brought onto the platform. It looked exactly like the Comte Du Barry.

"Why and how did you murder me, you despicable woman? I want you to reveal how you did it so that I can find peace at last," he screamed, pointing his finger at her.

"Put this man out of his misery and tell us how you murdered him and all the others. If you do help his soul to rest, you will redeem yourself and escape the horrible fate that awaits you. Speak," summoned the judge.

Marie started shaking with horror and fear when the man she killed only days before, appeared before her eyes.

"I will reveal my secret if it is the only way to save my soul," said Marie after a moment of hesitation.

"I wanted to find a way to avenge myself and all the other women who suffered at the hand of men without being caught. I had no intention to spend the rest of my days in prison or face the executioner.

"I sought the advice of a very well-known self-confessed witch whom I had consulted just before the authorities of the day condemned her to be burnt at the stake."

"Now tell us how did you do it," asked the judge raising his voice.

"Well first I would slip a special sleeping potion in their drink then, lying their head on my lap, I introduced a very long steel needle through one temple and retrieved it from the other temple without leaving a trace. Death was instantaneous. No one ever found out my secret and were able to condemn me," Marie said triumphantly.

"Now they have!" said Inspecteur Leblanc uncovering his face and slipping out of his robes.

"We put up this great performance just to have you believe you were dead and being judge by the Almighty. It was the only way to extract the truth from you."

"I saw le Comte du Barry here ... in this Court," stuttered Marie

"We made a death mask at the morgue and one of our men wore it to mislead you."

Marie suddenly fainted and collapsed on the floor and as the men rushed to pick her up to lay her on a bench, the blond wig she was wearing came off her head and fell on the floor. They brought over smelling salts and placed the bottle under her nose. She started coming to and opened her eyes.

"Where am I? Where are my children?" she murmured.

The inspecteur looked at her and understood. Violette had reappeared. Marie was gone hopefully for ever.

"It's a long story Madame Dulac. One of the men will take you home now and we will talk some other time."

"Yes, please take me home to my children."

Jenny Chevalier

Into me I see

For me intimacy has shifted, morphed, changed meaning.
It is wearing a new face.
Intimacy has become 'into me I see.'
I have created a world, a relationship within myself and now I don't want, desire or crave another.
I used to be scared of 'forever alone.'
Now I run from 'forever together.'
Til death do us part.
The idea of this IS death to me.
Empty promises of continued coupling combined with an unforeseeable future.
Feels like a formula for failure.
We are fickle.
We expect too much and offer too little.
We want more but give less.
We take and we take and we take.
Love burns out, yet we keep trying to light the sunken, shrivelled, scorched wick.
The flame is dead, so we soak it in a layer of lies and flick a match in its general direction – hoping for reignition, resulting in internal combustion.
What is left?
Smoke trails of love.
I reflect, I regroup, I rewrite.
I see in to me.
I find intimacy.
It is and always has been a part of me.
I complete me.

Jennifer Baker

How to exist

Put on a big coat when it's cold,
take it off in the sunshine. Balance your expectations
against those who mistrust you.
feed the birds, finish the laundry.
Ponder those skeletons found
in Pompeii. Develop delicate delineation dissertations,
remain aware of quiet inconsiderates.
Speak poorly of yourself,
speak poorly of others.
Eat water crackers when nauseous in the dead of night,
eat water crackers on the streets of Paris.
Hold yourself to only the things you can manage,
aspire to manage more.
Never forget everything happened to happen
to bring your happenings here.
What miracles did you eat for breakfast?
How long do you have?
What's to show for it?
Never ever lie when you say you love someone.
Never ever pass up the opportunity
to giggle in the snack isle of the supermarket.

Lucy Tomov

Music

There are two things you should know about me. I'm a teenager, and my Mum's music rules my life.

Just five minutes ago, when I was about to do my homework, the music began. I closed the book and waited to hear what kind of music she was going to play on the *Steinway* today. Straight away I recognised the vibrant sounds of Beethoven's *Emperor Concerto* filling the house. Stirring old memories.

I've come to know my Mum's moods by her playing. Is she sad, angry, or happy this time? Has Dad been drinking too much again, and hurt her? Maybe he's come home with flowers and kisses. He's just as unpredictable. The older I get the easier it is to read the signs.

My Mum's hands are broad and practical, with short square nails. *You can't have long nails to play the piano Emma,* she keeps telling me, so I pretend I don't see how she continually chews them raw. There are some things a kid shouldn't know, but you can't unlearn what you see, or feel, can you?

When I was little, she would say, *Come and play baby girl,* and she'd lift me up onto her lap. I'd put my hands over hers and we'd play together, running up and down the yellow keys till my fingers hurt. But I wouldn't tell her. And she'd tickle me, and we'd laugh. I remember she'd whisper stories in my ear, and we'd sing the French nursery rhymes she'd taught me. I was happy then. Safe. My brother Guy was alive then. Sometimes I'm angry with him getting sick and leaving me. He balanced us as a family. Sort of them and us. It's lonely being the only child. The twin left.

I wish she would change. Go out more. Smile more. Be happier. More like my school mates' cool mums. That would stop people talking. Embarrass me less. And I wish she'd stand up to Dad more. Sometimes I feel bad thinking these things. I want to help her. I hope I'll know how when I get older.

My Mum is her piano. The piano is my Mum. She's told me hundreds of times about her life in Europe, and the concerts she'd played in before meeting Dad. Long before Guy and I were born. Maybe she loved the freedom of that life more than the one she's got now.

But in the short time I've been talking to you, Mozart's softer music is beginning to flow through the house. This is a good sign. It's telling me she's feeling better. Calmer. And when I hear the bang of the piano lid closing, I know she'll come running down the hall to find me. She'll hug me, and tell me to leave my homework for there are better things to do. And everything will be ok again. Till the next time.

This is my roller coaster life, which I have no control over. For now. You can see that, can't you? Besides, I love my Mum more than anything, and soon we'll leave this house together. We'll go out into the sun. Play games. Have fun.

Sandra Lanteri

16,903.84

Sixteen thousand nine hundred three
and eighty-four hundredths kilometres
stretch between us—
an invisible thread pulled taut
from Melbourne's sunlit streets
to London's rain-soaked lanes,
where your morning meets my night.
Your day begins
when mine falls into shadow.
The time zones play tricks,
an ocean away,
while the echoes of your voice
fade with the distance
and the hum of cities.
I think of you under different skies,
the city lights of London
reflected in the Thames,
while I wander along the Yarra,
Each step we take,
separate but linked,
a map drawn in longing—
the world feels both vast
and unbearably small,
yet I carry you
in every corner of my heart.

Amanda Divers

My English teacher

He was my teacher of English and History for just a year
In a high school, a new school in my last year of school
He was a tall man, a passion for Australian literature
A friendly disposition he had
A good home life and happy in his job perhaps
I would sit in the front row and listen with attentive ears
He read from stories of old, stories of lives and land that were harder in some ways
My sense of loneliness was eased with the power of words
Awakening new ways of seeing the world
The world of words that bring new possibilities
So I would sit in the front row, not to miss a word
Sitting in the front row of a class I did not know
He read with a love for Australian Literature
Words that came to life with tone, expression and authenticity
Evoking a visual, sensory image in my mind
I admired his poise and presence
With love of performance, reading and acting out his particular role
He had won me over with words conveying the beauty of this land that the author loved so
I didn't understand the power of words and the magic of the landscape until later in life
So I would like to thank my English Teacher in my last year of school for introducing me to the
way of words
Thank you Mr Hosking

Rose Lumbaca Crane

The little things

As a baby I was easily delighted
Rattles, bright colors, peek-a-boo.
As a toddler even a cardboard box
Could fuel imaginary games.
Teen years saw the wanting setting in
Why can't I have this and that and those I whined.
Twenty something – mere excitement ruled
Parties, love affairs, what's next?
The short-lived thrill of acquisition
Houses, clothing, cars,
While travel ruled supreme:
What to plan, where to go?
Greek islands, tropical escapes
It was never enough.

And now, as life takes its toll
Joints creak, desires lessen
It's the little things that bring greatest joy:
The first pink blossom in late winter
A barely known neighbor brings homemade dumplings
Coffee and nostalgia with old friends
Just sitting with him, our fingers interlaced,
Laughing at some dumb old movie
And realizing this is enough
More than enough.

Sharon Hurst

Secrets of love

Rosa sits at her desk, surrounded by towering stacks of legal documents, her mind drifting away from the complex cases she is handling. Now in her late thirties, she has climbed the corporate ladder with unmatched determination, earning respect and success as a top lawyer in a major Melbourne company. Yet, her professional accomplishments seem to cast a shadow on her personal life. She doesn't have one.

Desperation lingers in her heart, a longing for a connection that transcends courtrooms and case files. She has, on numerous occasions, attempted to find love, but her impressive credentials often intimidate potential partners. Frustrated by this recurring pattern, Rosa makes an appointment with her analyst, Maxine Harper, to once again talk it through.

~~~

Rosa sits across from Dr. Harper in her cozy, dimly lit office. The faint hum of the air conditioner and the soft rustle of paper create a calming ambiance. Dr. Harper, a seasoned psychologist with kind eyes and a gentle demeanour, leans forward, ready to delve into the labyrinth of Rosa's emotions.

"Alright, Rosa," Dr. Harper begins, her notepad resting on her lap. "Let's talk about what's been on your mind lately."

Rosa takes a deep breath, her gaze fixes on a distant point in the room.

"It's this loneliness, Doc. It's suffocating, and I can't shake it off."

Dr. Harper nods, encouraging Rosa to continue.

"It's not that I don't have friends or a fulfilling career," Rosa explains. "But when it comes to romantic relationships, I can't seem to let anyone in. I've built this fortress around myself, and I don't know how to tear it down."

Dr. Harper leans back, crossing her legs and mirroring Rosa's calm disposition. "Let's explore that fortress, Rosa. What do you think keeps you from letting someone get close?"

Rosa sighs, her fingers absentmindedly tracing patterns on her notepad. "I guess I'm afraid of getting hurt, you know? The vulnerability that comes with opening up to someone feels like a weakness. And I've worked so hard to be strong, independent."

Dr. Harper nods in understanding. "It sounds like you've constructed this armoury to protect yourself. But tell me, Rosa, has it ever felt like it's keeping you prisoner too?"

Rosa's eyes flicker with a mix of recognition and contemplation. "Maybe... maybe I've been so focused on not getting hurt that I've closed myself off from potential connections. But it's hard to let go of that fear, Doc."

Dr. Harper leans forward; her voice gentle yet firm. "Facing that fear is the first step, Rosa. It's about finding a balance between protecting yourself and allowing others to see the real you. Vulnerability isn't weakness; it's the courage to be authentic."

Rosa nods, absorbing Dr. Harper's words. "I've also noticed that I avoid dating altogether. It's like I've convinced myself I'm better off alone."

"Let's explore that reluctance," Dr. Harper suggests. "What thoughts come up when you think about dating?"

Rosa hesitates before admitting, "I worry about losing control. What if I invest time and emotions into someone, and it all goes south? It's easier to stay in my comfort zone."

Dr. Harper nods seriously. "Control can be a safety net, but it's essential to acknowledge that not everything in life can be controlled. Sometimes, taking risks is what leads to the most rewarding experiences."

"I've also found the men that I'm interested in, get turned off by the fact that I'm a high-profile lawyer. They find it too intimidating."

Dr. Harper nods knowingly. "I think that here's your real problem."

"What should I do?"

"Let's discuss the possibilities in our next session. Maybe you could avoid telling the next random guy you link up with what you do."

As the session unfolds, Rosa begins to realize that there is more to all of this than peeling back the layers of her emotions and confronting her fears. The determined look in her eyes acknowledges the possibility of real change of approach.

As Dr. Harper escorts her to the door, she leaves Rosa with a smile.

"Rosa, remember, that true strength lies in vulnerability and that by embracing it in the right way, this might just be the key to breaking down the walls of your self-imposed fortress."

Back in the safety of her glass-towered fortress, Rosa makes a bold decision – she will create a secret identity on a dating site, portraying herself as a humble secretary seeking companionship.

Meanwhile, the hum of the city below echoes through the sleek glass windows of Rosa's corner office, a backdrop to her focused demeanour. The pile of papers on her desk, however, and the way she views them, indicates she knows she faces a challenge that will test her mettle.

The walls of her office are adorned with degrees, accolades, and framed victories. Yet, as Rosa studies the pile of legal documents on her desk, her thoughts are that her next battle will not be won with credentials alone.

The current case involves a high-stakes corporate merger, and the opposing counsel is no stranger to courtroom theatrics. The pressure is palpable, but Rosa thrives on the intensity of such challenges. She takes a sip of her espresso, the bitter warmth fuelling her determination.

The first step is to dissect the intricacies of the case. Rosa's fingers dance across the keyboard, accessing databases and legal resources with an ease born of countless hours spent navigating the labyrinth of jurisprudence. She isn't just a lawyer; she is a maestro orchestrating legal symphonies.

The clock ticks away as Rosa dives headlong into the sea of legal precedents, carving a path through the dense thicket of statutes and regulations. Her mind is a battlefield, with each argument a soldier meticulously prepared for the legal war ahead.

Rosa's phone buzzes, interrupting her immersion. It is a message from her associate, Alex, who seeks her guidance on a crucial aspect of the case. She responds with precision, weaving together legal principles and strategic insight. In her mind, every piece of advice is a chess move, a step closer to victory.

As the day unfolds, Rosa schedules a series of intense strategy sessions. Her conference room becomes a war room, where her team gathers to discuss tactics, brainstorm arguments, and anticipate the opponent's moves. Rosa blooms in the collaborative energy, drawing strength from the diverse perspectives of her handpicked team.

In the midst of this legal ballet, Rosa receives a surprise call from a key witness. Her ability to connect with people on a personal level is one of her secret weapons. In a conversation that feels more like a carefully choreographed dance, she extracts crucial information, leaving the witness feeling heard and understood.

Late into the evening, Rosa's office is a beacon of determination. The city lights shimmer beyond the windows as she meticulously crafts her legal brief. Every word is a strategic choice, a brushstroke on the canvas of her argument. Rosa knows that in the courtroom, eloquence is as potent as evidence.

The night air is crisp when Rosa finally closes her laptop. The legal battlefield is set, and she is confident that she has orchestrated a symphony of legal prowess. As she glances out at the city below, Rosa feels a surge of confidence. The tough assignment is now a challenge met, a testament to her unwavering tenacity and mastery of the law. She is sure that the next day in court will be the stage where she will once again showcase her prowess in the art of legal warfare.

Now back at home, the soft glow of Rosa's laptop bathes her in the only light in her dimly-lit apartment as she settles onto her lavish couch. Her fingers dance across the keyboard, navigating through a sea of online dating sites. In the digital realm of potential connections, she seeks a spark that might ignite the flame of romance.

Rosa is always known for her sharp intellect and unwavering confidence in the courtroom, but this is different. A totally unpredictable world of online dating. She feels a twinge of vulnerability that urges her to keep her true identity hidden. With a hint of mischief, she crafts her online persona, not as the fierce lawyer she is, but as a secretary – a role that allows her to blend into the crowd.

As she creates her dating profile, Rosa carefully selects the perfect pictures, each one capturing a different facet of her personality. A radiant smile in one, a contemplative gaze in another. She wants to present herself as approachable and genuine, keeping her legal prowess under wraps for now. The cursor hovers over the occupation section, and with a mischievous grin, she types 'Secretary' instead of 'Lawyer.'

Rosa leans back, sipping on a glass of red wine, as she admires her handiwork. It is a game, a chance to experience a different side of life. The thrill of the unknown mingles with the excitement of potential connections.

Night turns into morning as Rosa anxiously awaits the outcomes of her digital experiment. Messages and likes trickle in, each one a new opportunity to explore uncharted territory. It thrills her.

Rosa sets her alarm for an hour and sleeps soundly. She is lucky like that. A lot of her girlfriends often complain that they can't cat-nap at will. Rosa could always do it. A residue of long hours studying for her bar examinations and getting whatever sleep she could to get her through. It worked then, and it works now.

The alarm goes off and she is as fresh as a daisy. Coffee, toast and a shower and she is back in the zone. There is a case to be won.

The courtroom buzzes with tension, an invisible force that hangs thick in the air. Rosa wears a look of unyielding determination, and beside her is a team of legal minds, each one a pillar of support in this battle of wits. The stakes are high, and the opposing team formidable. It will be a tough day, a relentless clash of legal titans.

Rosa, dressed in her signature sharp suit, exudes confidence as she faces the judge, ready to navigate the complex web of arguments.

The opposition presents their case with calculated precision. The courtroom becomes a battlefield of words. As the day unfolds, legal jargon fills the room like a dense fog. Objections are raised, arguments countered, and evidence dissected in the intricate dance of litigation.

Hours pass, and the weariness of the courtroom battle etches lines on everyone's faces. Rosa's determination remains unyielding. She fights, not just for victory, but for the principles she believes in.

The judge's gavel echoes, signalling the end of the day's legal skirmish. Rosa's team retreats to a small conference room, a temporary refuge from the battlefield outside.

In the dimly lit room, amidst stacks of legal documents and empty coffee cups, Rosa rallies her team. Despite the absence of a clear winner, there is a collective sense of accomplishment, a shared acknowledgment that they have weathered the storm together. The walls might not have echoed with cheers of victory, but there is pride in knowing they have held their own against a formidable opponent.

"We may not have a clear win today, but we stood strong," Rosa declares, her eyes reflecting the fatigue of battle. "We defended our ground, and that's a victory in itself."

Her team nods in agreement; the camaraderie palpable in the room. The courtroom may have been a battleground, but here, in the aftermath, there is a sense of unity and resilience.

As they disperse, Rosa can't help but feel a surge of satisfaction. In the realm of law, and the demanding arena of the courtroom, victories are not always measured in clear-cut wins but in the ability to withstand the relentless challenges thrown their way.

There is no way Rose can face cooking alone so she arranges to meet a girlfriend, Louise, at a nearby café.

The aroma of garlic and simmering tomatoes envelopes Rosa and Louise as they sit in a dimly lit corner of La Trattoria, a quaint Italian restaurant tucked away from the bustling city streets. The soft glow of candlelight dances on their faces, casting a warm ambiance over the intimate setting.

Rosa stirs her spaghetti absentmindedly, the twirl of noodles reflecting the tangled thoughts in her mind. Louise, her girlfriend of only six months, sips on her martini, her eyes filled with curiosity as she gazes at Rosa.

"So, Rosa," Louise begins, her voice a gentle melody in the hushed atmosphere, "have you ever thought about going back to the world of men? You know, exploring that option again?"

Rosa looks up from her plate, a wry smile playing on her lips. "Louise, you know I've been there, done that. It's not about going back; it's about moving forward. Besides, I'm perfectly content with you."

Louise chuckles, her fingers tracing the rim of her glass. "Fair enough, we love each other's company and conversation, but we don't sleep together. Sometimes I wonder if we're missing out on something, or just copping out on life, by not tapping into the other side of the dating pool. Not that I want to, but you know, curiosity."

"Curiosity killed the cat, my dear," Rosa quips, lifting her wine glass in a mock toast. "Let's just stick to what we know for now."

"The simple fact is that we were both lonely and now we're not," says Louise quite casually.

Rosa nods in total acceptance.

The conversation then seamlessly shifts to the general topic of loneliness and the modern struggle to connect. They delve into the paradox of being more connected than ever through the internet while feeling a deeper sense of isolation. Rosa shares stories of her friends who, despite having hundreds of online friends, confess to feeling lonelier than ever.

"Isn't it ironic?" Rosa muses, swirling her wine. "We have the entire world at our fingertips, yet finding genuine connections is like searching for a needle in a haystack."

Louise nods, her eyes reflecting empathy. "It's the paradox of choice, I guess. Too many options can be paralysing. We're all swiping left and right, expecting a perfect match to magically appear."

They pause, a moment of reflection settling between them. The ambiance of the restaurant seems to amplify the solitude that lingers in their words.

"And don't get me started on the whole online dating scene," Rosa continues, a hint of frustration in her voice. "It's like a digital circus out there. People presenting curated versions of themselves, searching for an ideal that might not even exist."

Louise reaches across the table, her hand finding Rosa's. "But we found each other in this chaos. Isn't that something?"

A tender smile spreads across Rosa's face. "Indeed, it is, Louise. Maybe amidst the noise, we stumbled upon a rare and genuine connection. Even if it is non-sexual."

As they toast to their serendipitous encounter, the world outside the restaurant continues its chaotic dance. Rosa and Louise, wrapped in the warmth of companionship, smile tenderly at each other. Both women are totally convinced that theirs is a friendship that will stand the test of time.

Once home again, Rosa plonks herself down on the couch and switches her laptop on. There are messages galore from hopefuls, just like her.

She reads the various conversations, learning about the diverse array of individuals populating the online dating scene.

Among the sea of profiles, she stumbles upon a message that catches her attention. Stan, a charismatic entrepreneur with a passion for adventure. Rosa dips her toe further into the water and strikes up a conversation that quickly evolves beyond the standard small talk. Rosa finds herself drawn to his wit and charm, forgetting for a moment the fabricated identity she has woven.

As their virtual connection deepens, Rosa grapples with the revelation that she could very well develop genuine feelings for Stan. The lines between her online secretary persona and the accomplished lawyer blur, creating a delicate dance between truth and fiction.

Rosa decides it is enough for one night and says she will contact him in a couple of days' time.

Having then dreamt about Stan that night, she decides to go online again straight after work.

Shared interests and a mutual love for bad puns lead to late-night conversations that make Rosa feel like she's talking to an old friend. Stan's messages are filled with humour, charm, and an unexpected depth that intrigues her.

One evening, as they banter back and forth about their favourite movies and obscure hobbies, Stan types a question that sent a thrill down Rosa's spine: "What do you say we take this conversation offline? How about a real-life date?"

Her heart skips a beat, and Rosa hesitates for a moment. The idea of meeting someone in person is both exhilarating and nerve-wracking. After a brief internal debate, she replies with an enthusiastic, "Yes, let's do it!"

They settle on a trendy coffee shop in the heart of the city for their first date. Rosa spends the days leading up to it planning the perfect outfit and rehearsing potential conversation starters in her mind. The anticipation is palpable as she imagines what it will be like to finally meet Stan face-to-face.

The day of the date arrives, and Rosa finds herself nervously sipping her latte in the corner of the bustling coffee shop. The scent of freshly ground beans fills the air as she glances at her phone, checking for any updates from Stan.

Just as she is beginning to worry that he might not show, the door swings open, and there he is – Stan, with a friendly grin that mirrors his profile picture. Rosa feels a mix of excitement and relief as she stands to greet him.

Their conversation flows effortlessly, just like it did online. Stan's humour translates seamlessly into real-life banter, and Rosa finds herself laughing at his jokes with a genuine warmth that makes the initial awkwardness fade away.

As they chat about their lives, dreams, and everything in between, Rosa discovers new layers to Stan's personality that the digital realm hadn't fully revealed. There is a spark, a connection that transcended the pixels on the screen. The chemistry is undeniable, and the coffee shop hums with the energy of two people discovering something special.

Stan suggests they take a stroll through a nearby park after finishing their coffee. Under the soft glow of streetlights, they meander along winding paths, sharing stories and exchanging laughter. The city sounds fade into the background as they get lost in the rhythm of each other's company.

As the evening unfolds, Rosa realizes that this is more than just a date. It is an exploration of uncharted territories, a journey into the unknown. The initial nerves transform into a sense of comfort, and she finds herself opening up to Stan in ways she hadn't expected, but still hesitant to reveal her true identity.

They reach a quiet bench surrounded by blooming flowers, and as they sit side by side, Rosa feels a warmth spreading through her. Stan, too, seems to be captivated by the magic of the moment. Time seems to slow down as they share hopes, fears, and dreams under the canvas of the night sky.

As the evening comes to a close, Stan walks Rosa back to her car, and they exchange a lingering hug. With a promise to meet again, they part ways with a shared smile that echoes the unspoken understanding that something special has just begun.

And so, in the heart of a bustling city, Rosa and Stan's online connection has blossomed into a real-world romance, proving that sometimes, love can be found in the most unexpected places – even in the pixels of a dating app – even in the pretence of not being absolutely truthful. The feelings are truthful and real.

So it is that Rosa embarks on an unexpected journey – one that would challenge her perceptions of identity and love. Little does she know that the choices she made online will have far-reaching consequences, weaving a tapestry of emotions that transcend the boundaries of the virtual world.

Rosa finds Stan charming, witty, and seemingly oblivious to her true profession. Their connection flourishes over six months, a period of shared laughter, intimate conversations, and genuine affection. Rosa revels in the joy of being loved for who she is, not the intimidating lawyer she has become.

One fateful night, where anticipation of further lovemaking is ever-present in Rosa's mind, she sits across from Stan in their favourite dimly-lit bistro. He looks surprisingly teary, and she fears the tranquillity of their idyllic romance may be shattered. The air crackles with an unspoken tension as Stan, a seemingly perfect match for Rosa, starts to reveal the gnawing secret that lurks in the shadows of his past.

"Rosa," he begins, his voice a hesitant murmur, "there's something I need to tell you. Something that could change everything."

As he speaks, the weight of his words presses on Rosa's shoulders. Her eyes narrow in concern, sensing the storm that looms on the horizon. Stan lays bare the details of his financial transgressions, a web of tax discrepancies that threaten not only his financial stability but also his freedom. Rosa, her legal instincts awakening like a dormant beast, listens intently, her mind already racing to formulate a plan.

"Stan, could you let me look over the papers?"

"But what can you do that my legal team couldn't?"

"So, what do you have to lose?"

It is the innocent simplicity that melts his heart to go along with the idea. He pulls a big file of papers from his briefcase and hands them to her.

"I don't want to burden you with all of this," he blurts out.

"It is no burden," says Rosa as she takes the folder and places it under her chair. "Let's not spoil tonight with this. I'll take a look at it tomorrow and see if I can see anything. It will be my pleasure to help you through this, even if I can't solve your problems."

It is the caring way in which she speaks that puts Stan at ease, almost instantly.

"You are an angel; you know that don't you?"

The night finishes at his place and in the morning, Rosa goes off to work as she normally does.

In the days that follow, Rosa immerses herself in the dance of legal intricacies, her days a blur of statutes, codes, and consultations. She persuades Stan to let her handle the situation, assuring him that her skills reach beyond the realm of a mere secretary. Little does he know that Rosa is about to unleash her legal prowess in a way that will leave him awe-struck.

The tax department, known for its relentless pursuit of justice, initially meets Rosa's inquiries with scepticism. Yet, like a skilled chess player, Rosa moves her pieces with calculated precision. She navigates through the labyrinthine bureaucracy, presenting evidence, crafting arguments, and negotiating with a finesse that defies her seemingly unassuming demeanour.

To everyone's surprise, Rosa's legal finesse prevails against the bureaucratic behemoth. The tax department, relenting on their aggressive stance, gradually withdraw their claws. Stan, saved from the impending disaster that has loomed over him like a dark cloud, sits in awe of the capabilities of the woman he has often dismissed as a mere "secretary."

The once-tranquil rhythm of their romance, shattered by the revelation of Stan's hidden turmoil, finds a new cadence. Rosa's triumph in the face of legal adversity becomes a testament to the depths of her capabilities, turning her into an unexpected hero in Stan's eyes.

As the storm clouds of legal uncertainty dissipate, Rosa and Stan emerge on the other side, their bond forged anew in the crucible of adversity. The complexities of tax discrepancies have become a chapter in their shared history, a chapter marked not by the impending doom it threatened, but by the resilience and unexpected strength that Rosa has brought to the forefront.

In the soft glow of victory, Rosa and Stan clink their glasses, toasting to a love that has weathered the tempest and emerged stronger on the other side.

But secrets have a way of revealing themselves, and Stan's friend, Ben, grows suspicious. Unable to fathom how a mere secretary could achieve such a feat, he starts to delve into Rosa's background.

Ben turns up to Rosa's office in the city and confronts her with the fact that he knows who she is and doesn't want to see Stan hurt by it.

That night, at Stan's home, where he is hosting a party to

introduce Rosa to his friends, she ponders her decision to come clean. There are no easy ways to do it.

The air inside Stan's cozy apartment is filled with a mix of laughter, clinking glasses, and the aroma of a delicious homemade meal. The dinner party is in full swing, and Rosa finds herself surrounded by Stan's eclectic group of friends. As the evening unfolds, she can't help but appreciate the genuine connections and the warmth that fill the room.

Seated at the dinner table, Rosa steals glances at Stan from across the room, her heart brimming with affection. She marvels at the ease with which he navigates the social scene, making everyone feel at home. However, there is a secret she has been carrying, a truth she feels compelled to share before their relationship goes any deeper.

Amidst the lively conversations, Rosa catches the eye of Ben. There is a silent understanding between them, a shared acknowledgment of the unspoken truths beneath the surface. Rosa takes a deep breath, realizing that the time has come to lay bare her identity, to let the chips fall where they may.

As the night unfolds, Rosa excuses herself from the group, beckoning Ben to join her on the balcony. The night sky stretches above them, adorned with stars that seemed to twinkle knowingly. Rosa leans against the railing; her gaze fixed on the cityscape below.

"Ben," she begins, her voice steady but tinged with vulnerability, "I need to tell Stan; in fact I need to share the truth with everyone tonight."

Ben nods knowingly, his eyes reflecting a mix of empathy and understanding. "Rosa, I was wondering when you would get around to it. We all have our secrets. What matters is how we choose to face them."

In that moment, Rosa feels a surge of gratitude for the camaraderie she has found within this group of friends. With Ben by her side, she rejoins the party, mustering all her courage.

As the clock ticks towards midnight, Rosa calls for everyone's attention. The room husheds, the laughter fading into an expectant silence. She looks at Stan, their eyes locking in a shared moment of connection.

"I've been living a double life," Rosa confesses, her voice carrying across the room. "I'm not just a secretary. I'm a high-profile lawyer, with a life that exists beyond these walls."

The revelation hangs in the air, a palpable shift in the atmosphere. Stan's eyes widen with surprise, and the room collectively gasps. Rosa continues, baring her soul to those gathered.

"I wanted to be honest with all of you, with you, Stan, because what we have is special. I didn't want any more secrets between us."

Silence envelops the room as the weight of Rosa's words settle in. Stan, after a moment of processing, approaches her with a gentle smile, reaching for her hand.

"Rosa," he says, his voice filled with a quiet strength, "I appreciate your honesty. What matters to me is the person you are, not the titles you hold. Let's navigate this together, whatever it may mean."

The room erupts into a mix of applause and supportive murmurs, the bonds of friendship proving stronger than any revelation. Rosa feels a weight lift off her shoulders, realizing that honesty has strengthened the connections around her.

When the party concludes, Stan and Rosa, hand in hand, say goodnight to the last guest.

Stan loosens his grip on Rosa's hand and she sees tension in his eyes.

"I thought as much, even though I didn't want to believe it," his words calm and direct. "You must have thought I was so gullible."

"Stan, you have no idea how many times I wanted to tell you and how many times I refused because I felt you would not love me anymore," pleads Rosa. "What we have is too special for me. I love you."

"I love you too. Or I thought I did."

"I'm begging for forgiveness for my deception. Let our love for each other be the force that wins the day."

As the city lights flicker outside Stan's apartment window, a heavy silence hangs in the air. The revelation about Rosa's deception weighs on Stan like a ton of bricks, casting a shadow over the love they have built together. The room, so recently filled with laughter and shared secrets, now feels cold and unfamiliar.

Stan sits on the edge of the couch, running his fingers through his dishevelled hair, his mind swirling with conflicting emotions. He can't shake the sense of betrayal that clings to Rosa's actions, no matter how hard he tries. The walls of trust they have carefully built seem to crumble with each passing moment.

Rosa, sensing the gravity of the situation, sits across from Stan, her eyes searching his face for any sign of forgiveness. The air is thick with unspoken words, as they both grapple with the painful reality of their unravelling relationship.

Stan finally speaks, his voice a mixture of disappointment

and hurt. "I thought we had something real, Rosa. I trusted you, when you couldn't trust me with your honesty."

Rosa's gaze drops, her shoulders slumping under the weight of guilt. "Stan, I never meant to hurt you. I did it because I thought I was protecting you. I love you."

The words hang in the air, but Stan's heart, wounded and weary, finds little solace in them. The foundation of their love have been shaken, and the cracks are too deep to mend with mere words.

A heavy sigh escapes Stan's lips as he leans back, the distance between them growing. "Love is built on trust, Rosa. And I can't trust you anymore. You saved me from going to jail, but you've cost me my peace of mind."

The admission hangs in the air, a painful truth that neither of them can escape.

Stan's decision to end the relationship feels like a heavy blow, the weight of which settles over the room like a shroud. Rosa's eyes well up with tears, her attempts to hold them back futile.

"I never meant for it to end like this," Stan says, his voice softer now, carrying the weight of his own sorrow. "But I can't be with someone I can't trust. It's over, Rosa."

As the finality of his words sink in, a profound silence envelops the room. The echoes of a love that once burned brightly linger in the air, now reduced to smouldering embers. Stan and Rosa, two souls who had found solace in each other's company, now face the painful reality of going their separate ways.

The city outside continues to buzz with life, unaware of the heartbreak unfolding within the confines of Stan's apartment. Love, once a beacon of hope, has become a casualty of deception, leaving both Stan and Rosa to navigate the wreckage of what was once their shared world.

Rosa stands up and allows Stan to see the hurt in her. So strong as a lawyer, she now feels weak and fragile. She can see that there was a rationale for what she did, in her mind, but there was no getting past it.

Rosa, a sombre silhouette against the muted hues of the dimly-lit apartment. Stan watches her, his normally sharp eyes softened by a mixture of concern and curiosity. The palpable silence between them is broken only by the distant hum of the city outside, a stark contrast to the emotional tempest within the four walls.

Rosa's usually composed demeanour has given way to vulnerability, her steely facade unravelling like a carefully crafted tapestry being unravelled thread by thread. She meets Stan's gaze, and in that fleeting moment, he catches a glimpse of the hurt etched across her face, a pain that transcends the polished exterior of the accomplished lawyer he now knew she was.

For someone accustomed to battling in courtrooms, Rosa feels defenceless in this personal confrontation. It is as if the armour she wears in her professional life has crumbled away, revealing the raw and tender humanity beneath. The weight of unspoken words looms heavily between them.

As she stands there, vulnerable yet resolute, Rosa realizes the futility of arguing her case. The logic that had guided her actions now seems feeble in the face of the emotional wreckage she has inadvertently caused. In her mind, there was a rationale, a twisted path of reasoning that justified her choices, but deep down, she understood that logic alone couldn't mend the emotional fractures that now separated them.

A heavy sigh escapes Stan's lips, his shoulders slumping. The room seems to close in around them, walls bearing witness to a moment of profound change.

With a subtle nod, Rosa concedes defeat in the unspoken battle. There is no need for words; they linger in the silence, heavy with unspoken apologies and the echoes of what once was. The inevitability of the situation settles like dust in the air, leaving behind a sense of resignation.

Stan, grappling with the realization that some wounds run too deep for reconciliation, offers a faint, understanding smile. It is a bittersweet acknowledgment of their shared time together that has already reshaped them.

In that final scene, as Rosa and Stan stand on opposite sides of an emotional chasm, the unspoken understanding becomes the punctuation mark to a chapter that has reached its melancholic conclusion.

Rosa leaves the apartment with a faint, unrealistic wish that, in some period of time to come, Stan might reconsider.

Back home, Rosa sees another message from a potential suitor seeking a secretary. Deleting it from her laptop, and then pouring herself a Napoleon Cognac, she resigns herself to not hearing from Stan again.

In her mind now, there is no way to go back and recreate what was. The magic would never be the same.

How could it?

Peter Levy

www.ingramcontent.com/pod-product-compliance
Lightning Source LLC
Chambersburg PA
CBHW062035290426
44109CB00026B/2636